Evolutionary Emergence
of Purposive Goals and Values

Evolutionary Emergence of Purposive Goals and Values

A Naturalistic Teleology

DONALD A. CROSBY

SUNY
PRESS

Cover image from Shutterstock

Published by State University of New York Press, Albany

© 2023 State University of New York

For information, contact State University of New York Press, Albany, NY
www.sunypress.edu

Library of Congress Cataloging-in-Publication Data

Name: Crosby, Donald A., author.
Title: Evolutionary emergence of purposive goals and values : a naturalistic teleology / Donald A. Crosby.
Description: Albany : State University of New York Press, [2023] | Includes bibliographical references and index.
Identifiers: ISBN 9781438493978 (hardcover : alk. paper) | ISBN 9781438493985 (ebook)
Further information is available at the Library of Congress.

10 9 8 7 6 5 4 3 2 1

Contents

Contents

Acknowledgments

I am grateful to copyeditor Dana Foote for keen attention to details in correcting matters in, or suggesting changes to, the earlier draft of this book. I thank Michael Rinella and Diane Ganeles and others at SUNY Press for their courteous, patient work in producing the contents and design of the book. I thank Michael Goldstein for preparing the Index. I am also indebted to author Mikael Leidenhag for his insightful challenges to my ways of thinking about issues relating to teleology. We do not agree in a number of details, but I hope that our disagreements can serve to enrich further thinking about this important topic. Finally, I thank my wife Pamela Crosby for her help in reading over each of the book's chapters with me, catching grammatical mistakes, noting unclarities in writing, and questioning my arguments at critical junctures. She is my indispensable grammarian, stylist, and hermeneut.

Introduction

There are many different interpretations of the character, value, and importance of the natural world. Some interpreters see it as a perilous, tragic, disappointing place and spend their lives yearning for God to rescue them from the world and speed them to a perfect heaven. In some cases, this outlook is prompted by harsh experiences of injustice, suffering, deprivation, and despair. In others, it is perhaps an inability or unwillingness to recognize or accept the inevitable ambiguities and limitations of finite existence. Some conclude that the world is meaningless if it is not believed to be created by a personal God who imparts to it an overarching purpose or set of purposes for its existence. Some accept willingly the idea that the natural world is devoid of intrinsic value and devote their lives to exploiting it for their own benefit in whatever ways possible.

And some who have come to reject belief in such a God conclude regrettably that whatever purpose, meaning, or value the world is to have for them must be created arbitrarily and at first hand by their own personal decisions. The world means, in other words, whatever humans individually or collectively *decide* for it to mean in the way of importance and value. The world is nothing other than a blank slate onto which humans have to project and inscribe their own purposes. Thus the world means for them conceptually and existentially whatever they take it to mean or wish for it to mean, in an unconstrained, purely subjective manner. Implicit in this last view is the idea that the only beings capable of telic or end-oriented actions that can regulate and guide the uses of freedom are humans themselves. Since the world has no inherent purposes or values in itself, or so the reasoning goes, it is up to humans to confer such purposes and values on it by arbitrary, unguided human decisions and actions.

But is a world bereft of intrinsic meaning the only alternative to a world given its fundamental purpose by God? Panpsychists of various stripes do not all accept this conclusion. The view of the nontheists among them (and many *are* theists) is that *psyche*, that is, mind or spirit, is primordial. It is part of the universe at the very outset of its coming into being, meaning that it does not depend on emergence over long periods of time. Mind is as basic as any other aspect of the universe, present in it from its very beginning, and possibly in earlier universes as well, throughout all time. Mind *guides* evolution on earth and elsewhere, and is not the *outcome* of evolution. It is why life forms, with either their reflexive or intentional modes of behavior, exist. Their end-oriented reflexive or conscious actions stem from the primordial factor of mind always resident in nature.

Therefore, natural life forms or organisms do not bring telic, end-oriented, purposive actions into the world. The ends or values of the world are always there, awaiting recognition and response from living beings. They also are not products of evolution but prior to it and what ultimately guide its developments. Without such assumed guidance, proponents of panpsychism assert, the evolutionary process itself would be neither explicable nor intelligible. Mental or psychic purposes, ends, and values have everywhere and always been present in nature; hence the essential *pan* ("all") part of the term *panpsychism*. Psychic phenomena are timeless and primordial. They are not late-arriving outcomes of the history of the earth. That history only brings into greater prominence mental factors active in it from the beginning.

My own view, which I shall explain and defend throughout this book, is that telic phenomena and the ends and values associated with them are without exception *emergent* factors in the history of the earth. They are preceded by the temporal comings into being of new *real* possibilities, not by antecedently unrealized *pure* ones, and these real possibilities are themselves gradually produced over immense stretches of time. Therefore, telic phenomena are neither de novo nor primordial. The primordial factors or principles required for explaining their eventual emergence are two and only two: *matter-energy and time.* The interactions of these two bring continuing genuine novelty into the world, and two of the most striking of its novel emergent results are first, *life* and later, increasingly *conscious* kinds of life. All forms of life are teleological, I shall argue, and conscious life is most conspicuously so. The world, in my view, has no antecedent, overall, general purpose for its being. Instead, it is the ground of and source for temporally emergent purposes. There is no overarching, single purpose of the world as a whole, but a plethora of emergent and active purposes currently here on earth and probably elsewhere in the universe as well.

The presence of purposive responses, experiences, and actions in the world does not require their bestowal by God with an original single, all-encompassing act of creation. Nor does it require assumption of psyche, spirit, or mind as primordial components of the world. The current presence of these realities is a creation of nature itself and is as real as anything else in nature. It is possible to subscribe to such a view and continue to believe in God, but it would be the God responsible for creating a nature that has this creative potential *within itself*, gradually bringing telic and mental phenomena into being by the twin agencies of matter-energy and time. In either event, telic phenomena would need to be regarded as processive *outcomes* rather than as *preconditions*. No primordial, implicitly incoherent mind-matter dualism would in either case be needed so far as the earth is concerned.

There would still remain the problem for the theist of conceiving a *purely spiritual* God without being able satisfactorily to explain the alleged relations of such a God to a pervasively *physical* earth and to living beings as products of the physical earth. As a religious naturalist who focuses his religious faith entirely on nature itself, I can leave it to thoughtful theologians to tell us how they think the formidable problem of a seemingly intractable God-world dualism can be most convincingly resolved. My conviction is that all reality is natural reality. And whatever is to be explained can only be—and need only be—explained or accounted for in naturalistic ways. This "only," however, leaves room for vast areas of fascination, wonder, perplexity, and mystery.

What I have offered so far here, however, is only a brief and in many ways vague sketch. It will have to be filled in with further elaboration, explication, and argument. It is the skeleton of a religious naturalist's interpretation of teleological phenomena that will need much fleshing out. Teleology is my focus throughout, and the key term *teleology* can best be explained by noting its etymology. The Greek word *telos* (plural: *telē*) means "end," or "goal." In some contexts, it can also be rendered as "purpose." And the attached word *logos* can, for our purposes, mean something like "study of," "reasoning behind," or even "logic of." *Teleology*, then, is the study of telic, or end-oriented and directed phenomena, with the hope of providing coherent, convincing general explanations for their presence in the world.

Such a study or inquiry need not assume that the world must have some kind of all-comprehending purpose. It can be satisfactory to conclude that all purposes are *in* the world, not *of* the world, meaning that none need apply to the world conceived as some kind of whole system that contains all other subsystems. The world gives every appearance to me, as

I shall demonstrate later, of being a pluriverse rather than a universe, in the etymological senses of these two words. A multitude of internal telic phenomena, each linked to many others but not to all others, need not presuppose a telos of the whole.

A world with a plethora of internal purposes, meaning, and values available to our contemplation and exercise is, in my way of thinking, an amply satisfying and fulfilling world. Such a world can be this for us despite all of its frightening and uncertain ambiguities. It does not center on us humans, but it can succor and sustain us even in the face of its enormity of scope, and of its necessary extensive order that enables it to be a cosmos rather than a mere aggregation and shamble of particular modes of being. But *kosmoi*, namely, the Greek term for a collection of interconnected but not necessarily finally hierarchically arranged, completely interdependent orders, makes the idea more plain. Throughout the universe (or, more properly, *pluriverse*), there are elements of autonomy combined with elements of interdependence.

This picture is part of the fascination, wonder, and daunting sublimity of a multifaceted, many-splendored world. It must also be accompanied by acknowledgment of the world's uneven distributions of tribulations and trials for its finite beings, and for some of them—human or nonhuman—much more so than for others. Such inequitable features of the finite world are outcomes of its vastness and pervasive contingencies, while others sadly result here on earth from ruthless or uncaring human choices. We humans must find ways to live in the face of the first, while constantly searching for ways to avoid the second—for the sake of ourselves as humans as well as for the other creatures of the earth. Ours is a world interlaced with tragedy and uncertainty as well as with confidence and hope.

I shall soon move on from this introduction to the book's main body, but first I want to offer a description of each of its seven chapters in order to give an initial idea of their contents and of how they, as the principal parts of the book, are connected with one another. My major focus here, however, shall be on the first chapter, since it gives a picture of six options for explaining or at least addressing the psychic phenomena that shall occupy us in the book. The sixth one of these options is my own. Having done so, I shall move to a briefer introduction to the other six chapters.

The first interpretation in chapter 1 is that of the French existentialist philosopher Jean-Paul Sartre. Sartre assumes that there is no such being, presence, and power as God and no creation of the universe by God. In the absence of God, he reasons, there is no such thing as a purpose of the world as a whole and no such thing as divinely ordered and prescribed meanings and values placed by God in the world.

There is also no such thing as a common human nature with obligations and expectations implanted in them as creations of God. They are not like manufactured goods with previously conceived and assigned purposes. Each human being is left entirely to itself when it comes to ends or purposes of human thought and behavior. Ends and values appropriate to human life are arbitrary and must be created from the outset by each and every human by naked and unassisted, arbitrary and undirected acts of the human will. We must each choose our own personal *telē* without any hope of assistance, assurance, or guarantee.

We are telic beings with absolute freedom of choice when it comes to such matters. But we are also abandoned and alone, and it is entirely up to each of us to go about deciding what we ought to aspire toward and how we ought to live. Our ends are our creations alone and not God's. They are also not assisted or warranted by nature because, for Sartre, nature is riddled with arbitrariness, contingency, and sheer openness of possibility.

At the other extreme from Sartre are traditional theists who believe that the world is a purposeful creation by God that gives abundant purposes to human life. And God makes known to humans in many ways, including direct revelations, what these purposes are and how they can be accomplished. Moreover, the nonhuman realm itself is a creation by God, with multiple evidence of God's purposeful intention and design. The world contains implicit values, meanings, and purposes inviting human response. It is a vast telic arena, and its telic ends are everywhere to be sought and found. It is such because it and everything in it invites and awaits responsible human choices. The second teleological interpretation sketched in this book's initial chapter, therefore, is that humans are not abandoned or alone. They can live their lives with confident reliance of the ends, values, and purposes God has designed and made available to them.

In the case of Sartre, as we just saw, ends lie nowhere but in the goals envisioned by isolated human beings. They, and they alone, are the sources and arbiters of telic phenomena. There are no intrinsic purposes or goals in an absurd and meaningless world. Only in humans are psychic concepts, aspirations, and behaviors to be found, and these are nothing other than expressions of an absolute, unguided, and unconstrained human freedom. For traditional theists, however, abundant telic goals are implanted in them and throughout nature by God. These goals can be aspired toward and achieved through the gracious help of God. Sartre's is a bleak, forlorn, and solitary picture of humanity, while traditional theism centers on an assumed benevolent God, creator of the universe and everything in it. Humans possess a divinely constituted common nature. Such a telic world elicits individual, communal, and confident response. It lays out the scope and character of human freedom, while Sartre's view of the world does not.

But theism also requires for its defense of panpsychism belief in the existence of God, belief in God's creation of the world, confidence in the goodness of God despite all of the perils, ambiguities, and uncertainties of the world, and an intelligible account of God's relations to and activity within the world. Psyche or spirit is assumed by most versions of theism to be the ultimate source of everything in the world. Not only are matter-energy and time given a secondary role, but it is not clear how a purely spiritual God, thought to exist beyond the conditions and constraints of time, could have intelligible relations to the pervasively physical and temporal character of the world.

The third option laid out in this book's first chapter for interpreting telic phenomena is eliminative, mechanistic materialism. This option is eliminative because it reduces everything to the level of physics, and it is mechanistic because it discounts the possibility of anything that cannot be accounted for in mathematical, strictly causal ways. What may look like human actions directed toward optional ends or goals are in reality no less causally determined, predictable, and constrained—at least in principle—than the functions of a highly developed machine. Teleology is reduced to or eliminated in favor of extremely complex modes of mechanistic behavior. No matter what things may look like or how they may feel, this is what they all amount to. What cannot be accounted for in a strictly scientific manner, and reduced finally to the domain of high-level mathematical physics, does not exist.

This statement would include Sartre's absolute freedom and the traditional theist's purely spiritual God. Chemistry, biology, psychology, the whole of human culture from its earliest time to the present, are reducible from seeming quality to pure quantity, and from a future with various possibilities open to different choices to one confined to inevitable, causally controlled ones. Humans themselves are robots or complex computers, and the world is one vast machine. Or alternatively, the world can be rightly viewed as a massive logical system or set of mathematical, deductive premises and conclusions awaiting analysis. There are no novelties anywhere, except what seem to be such from our limited and entirely mistaken human perspectives. Efficient causes are both necessary and sufficient conditions for any occurrence.

Time itself is devoid of novelty. It rolls relentlessly on, its every moment completely predictable at least in principle, and its future already completely contained in its past. In this eliminative, mechanistic perspective, there are no teleological, end-directed phenomena requiring explanation. Thus teleology is not so much explained as explained away. And the open future that teleology would seem to require is reduced to a future that simply replicates or reenacts what is already implicitly contained in its past. Not only is a credible role for teleology eliminated, so too is a credible account of the flow of time and of the very meaning of time.

The fourth, fifth, and sixth ways of interpreting teleological phenomena I present and discuss in chapter 1 are the way of the American philosopher Thomas Nagel, that of the English philosopher Alfred North Whitehead, and my own way of doing so. Nagel defends panpsychism, or the primordial, original, underived presence of directing mind in nature. And he does so without appeal to the existence of God. Whitehead defends a version of panpsychism or panmentalism by arguing that each of the basic units of reality has a "bipolar" character composed of an interlinked physical and a mental aspect. I, on the other hand, deny that mind is primordial, arguing instead that it is emergent, requiring a prolonged evolutionary time to become present in various developing forms on earth. I champion an emergentist source for teleology without making reference to God, thus agreeing with Nagel only in the latter respect. I do so as a religious naturalist whose focus of religious faith is on nature itself rather than on belief in God.

Nagel defends the thesis that there are teleological laws operative in the universe as complements to its efficient causal ones. Acceptance of such laws is necessary if we are to give a satisfactory account of biological evolution. They are necessary preconditions for the evolution of mind rather than being emergent products of it. The staggering intricacy and complexity of the processes of biological evolution demand for him such preconditions, an operative aim and direction already present in every stage of evolution. He is convinced, therefore, that my two sole primordials of matter-energy and time would be insufficient to explain teleological phenomena, even with long expanses of time and a crucial role of chance or novelty factored in. Whitehead's metaphysics is based on the conviction that the world is a blend of dependence on the past and purposive movement into the future, and that his actual entities (or actual occasions) are required to explain why this is so. He also gives a prominent role to God in explaining how this is so, but his God—unlike the traditional theistic one—did not create the world and needs it as much as the world needs God.

I do not need to belabor my own view of teleology at this point, since this book as a whole is principally dedicated to its development and defense. Suffice it to say that I do hold that time is real, that novelty is an essential factor in the working of time, that matter-energy is dynamic and protean, that human freedom is real and not just a mechanistic process, and that the mind has a genuinely qualitative character throughout, meaning that its firsthand experiential qualities cannot be successfully explained as mere epiphenomenal illusions or reduced to something purely quantitative and mechanical.

Especially crucial to my teleological theory is the reality of time. Time for me makes tremendous differences over its extremely long stretches because time is a combination of continuity and novelty, and the novel factor in its flow becomes increasingly important and constitutive of material reality as that reality extends into the future. Time moves relentlessly forward and cannot be wound backward. This means that the present cannot be reduced to the past and that the future cannot be reduced to the present. Mine is thus a radically *non-eliminative* form of materialism because of its insistence on a central role for novelty in the ongoing history of the world and on the presence of teleological phenomena—that is, forms of life here on earth—as the outcome of well over three billion years of that history, starting with extremely simple anaerobic types of life.

I regard all life as teleological in the sense that all of it has at least to some degree a built-in orientation and directedness toward future ends. In doing so, I follow the lead of Evan Thompson. In his book *Mind in Life*, Thompson makes a convincing case for the thesis that all forms of life have the three basic, interconnected traits of *autopoiesis* (self-making), *sensation* (sense making), and *purposiveness* (future-oriented adaptive behavior in relation to aspects of a life form's natural environment). These three traits entail what Thompson calls "the deep continuity of life and mind" (2007: 157; see especially 157–62). What this idea amounts to is that teleology makes its first appearance on earth with the evolution of life and continues to this day to be a property of all forms of life, including our own.

Agreement with Thompson in this respect is essential in my approach to teleology. I have found no reason for thinking that Nagel would disagree with some of my convictions despite my strong disagreement with his version of panpsychism. He is staunchly opposed to eliminative materialism, for example, although for a reason different from my own. Nevertheless, this difference in reasoning is fundamental and far-reaching, as is our disagreement about the nature of teleology itself. Nagel's view is similar in many ways to that of the Swedish philosopher Mikael Leidenhag, whose extended arguments in favor of panpsychism I take into consideration and challenge in much of chapter 5.

Moving now to chapter 2, the two meanings of *telos* I explore there are those of the ancient philosopher Aristotle. The first meaning is that of the end or outcome regularly achieved by some kind of natural process. An egg becomes a chicken, an acorn becomes an oak, or an embryo becomes a child, for example. In similar fashion, the sun and the moon are thought by him to circle the earth, their regular circuiting orbits being their natural ends. There is no suggestion of purpose in these processes. They are not for Aristotle the creations of an intentionally purposive God.

The other sense of *telos* has to do with some sort of purposive behavior, and it is the focus of this second chapter. In its most basic form, as I have argued earlier, it is a property of all life, but not necessarily as a kind of consciously intended action or behavior, a capability that emerges only with more complex forms of life on earth.

Nature as a whole has a *telos* for Aristotle but does not have such by virtue of being created by a conscious God. It is not the product of purposeful creation. In fact, the world for Aristotle has always existed. He has no concept either of its creation or of its evolution. His Unmoved Mover is simply the form or actuality of the whole, that is, the end it exhibits in its profusion of regular, orderly, predictable processes and changes. But his idea of the whole of nature as having no kind of *purposive* end was transmuted later by Jewish, Christian, and Islamic theologians and interpreters of Aristotle into its being the creation of a personal God who gives intended purpose to every aspect of the world in the act of creation. In this way, versions of theistic panpsychism have been developed, partly on the basis of Aristotelian philosophy.

This interpretation of Aristotle is mistaken, showing in one important way why it is important to distinguish the two senses of *telos* and, by implication, two very different approaches to teleology. Nature has as many kinds of immanent purposes as are implicit in the modes of action and behavior of its many types of life, but it has no overall purpose, as I have already indicated. Its sole *preconditions* are matter-energy and time, and neither is a conscious agent. They eventually produce life on earth, but conscious life takes an extremely long time to evolve from the innumerable earlier unconscious but also teleological forms of it.

I go into some detail in this second chapter describing the stages of this evolutionary process. In doing so, I emphasize the distinction between "how" questions and "why" questions. There is no meaningful answer, in my view, to the question of *why* the evolution of life and its teleological character has occurred on the face of the earth. The only possible answer is just that this has been nature's way of doing things, an answer that leads directly to the more answerable question of *how* it does so. And that, in my judgment, is where our investigations should be directed. I focus throughout the chapter on the how question and include in my discussion attention to the adaptive values of conscious types of life, paying special attention to conscious human life in this regard.

In doing so, I set forth a view of the status of values, their adaptive ends with respect to aspects of a creature's natural environment and in relation to the social lives of human beings. I argue that values should not be conceived so much as independently resident in nature but as existing in the relations of living beings, and especially conscious ones like us, to aspects of the world. Values have a vector character. They are experienced here as about something there. What may have the value of food from one aspect may have the value of an inviolable thing of beauty from another. What may constitute a home for one creature may be construed merely as a tree from another. What may be seen as a friend from one perspective can be regarded as an enemy from another. And so on. Value, disvalue, and teleology are inseparably bound together. No valuative ends to be sought for, no teleology. No teleology, no such thing as values.

Everything necessary for the telic functioning of any organism is experienced as such from its perspective and for its purposes. And everything that functions in this manner for the organism is thereby constituted as a value or disvalue for it. In looking at the matter in this way, I contend that I do not commit some kind of "is-ought" or "naturalistic" fallacy. That is, I do not claim that the mere act of valuing creates genuine values. Values are potentially present as discoverable facts of nature, but they exist as such only in their relations to telic beings. Were there no telic beings, there would be no values.

But it is also true, I hold, that there would be no such thing as facts. What count as facts count as such from the perspectives of beings capable of recognizing, naming, or responding to them as such. The world is through and through an *interpreted* world, both in the way of putative values and in the way of putative facts. The role of teleology is implicit in both ways of thinking about it. I defend at length a version of this crucial idea of the world as an interpreted world in an earlier book (Crosby 2022b; see especially chapter 7).

The theme of the essential connection between teleology and values is taken up again in chapter 3. There I discuss four types of positive values we humans discover in our relations to the world. The first is the value we naturally feel toward ourselves and for the preservation, prolongation, and enhancement of our personal lives. The second is the values we find and urgently require, as naturally social beings, in our relations with others. These values can and should extend from our fellow humans to all of the sentient beings with whom we share our lives in this planet. The third is the captivating values we discern in the earth, sea, and sky of our remarkable home planet. And the fourth is the values pertaining to the sacred majesty of the massive universe (or pluriverse) of which planet earth is but a tiny part. In the broadest possible perspective, we earthlings and our planet are to the enormity of the universe what a microbe is to the earth as a whole.

All such values, whether relatively minor or inexpressively sublime, can have either explicit or implicit moral, aesthetic, and religious import. And they can elicit the unending fascination and wonder of scientists, philosophers, and other committed inquirers as they strive for a greater, more comprehensive, more liberating and healing understanding of our human selves and of our world. Teleology and its necessarily accompanying values are no less grand and amazing subsequent outcomes of an evolved and continuously evolving nature than they would be as something always and everywhere primordial and underived.

Chapter 4 continues on this path of observation and analysis by stressing the interconnections of causality and contingency that have made the evolution of the universe and of the earth to date. Causal relations provide a basis of continuing order for the ongoing work of novelty or chance to do its work. On earth, the result of these two factors, in their necessary dependence on the more ultimate inherent powers of matter-energy and time, has been the universe as we experience and regard it today, and especially the closer-to-home marvels of extensive terrestrial development and change, including the evolution of teeming numbers of diverse kinds of living beings with their widely varying teleological capacities and powers.

So extensive is the teleological power of human freedom, accompanied by the remarkable potencies of the human mind, that the fate of the earth is today direly threatened by human freedom's past misdirections and misuses and by its continuing destructive effects for the earth itself and all of its creatures, including its human ones. This is the ecological crisis of our time. I attend first in the chapter to the fate of the earth itself and its nonhuman creatures, and second to the fate of us human beings, as these two aspects of earth continue to be increasingly and even exponentially affected by human choices or failures of choice, and their resulting actions or inactions. The crucial importance of teleology is underscored by the urgency of this crisis. The reality of human freedom and our capabilities as intelligent beings give assurance that we are capable of dealing effectively with this ever-growing crisis. So it does not have an already fated or determined outcome. But commendable and hopeful resolution of it will require maximum concentration and use of our cooperative imaginations and powers of thought, planning, and will. I discuss three commonplace miracles present on earth today in order to provide assurance of our ability to meet the challenge of the crisis, but only to the extent that we proceed immediately to actualize and enforce them.

The first miracle is the primordial creative power of matter-energy and time that has produced us as creatures with an extraordinary amount of intellectual acumen, genuine freedom, and actionable capability. We are material beings who can join our own creative abilities with those of nature, and do so in ways that contribute to nature's wellbeing on earth in the helpful, constructive, comprehensive ways needed for rising to the challenge of the current ecological crisis. The other two miracles are the evolution of life itself and, with it, the evolution of conscious forms of life, including our own.

We are outcomes of evolution, and the powers it has conferred on us have now paradoxically become severe threats to the integrity of parts of the earth such as its sky, oceans, and land, to the continued flourishing of its nonhuman creatures in their natural environments, and to our own flourishing and long-range survival as one of its innumerable creatures. The stupendous responsibility this inescapable fact imposes on us humans today cannot be ignored, postponed, or set aside. We can meet the challenge of this crisis by drawing on faith in the resilience of nature and our awesome adaptive capabilities as creatures of nature. And we can best do so, in my considered judgment, by placing aspects of both our secular and religious faiths in nature and in the extraordinary powers conferred on us by nature.

Nature on earth in some shape and form will probably survive even our worst travesties, but we and countless other natural beings may not survive if we fail to do our necessary part as humans today. Like all natural beings, we depend crucially on nature here on earth, but it is becoming increasingly evident that the prosperity of earth and of large numbers of its other evolved creatures depend crucially on us. We have the urgent responsibility of putting our naturally evolved powers to work, not only in service to one another but in service of other evolved creatures and their interdependent ecosystems on earth, of which we humans are integral parts and on which we vitally depend. The immediate full recognition and effective utilization of our telic powers is the issue of greatest moment confronting human civilization today. Viewed in this way, the topic of teleology comes to have an overwhelmingly relevant importance it might seem to lack when approached and regarded only in a detached, abstract manner. Chapter 4 is designed to bring this message home.

The last section of the fourth chapter underlines this point by noting that the ultimate authority to which appeal must be made in dealing with the current ecological crisis, our roles as creatures of an evolved and evolving nature, and our profound responsibility to our natural home *lies in our interpretations of nature and of our perceived place in nature*. There are many religious traditions that take fundamentally into account the truth of the *sacredness* of nature itself and of every aspect of nature—whether this truth is traced to divine creation and maintenance of the natural order or simply to the inherent creative and sustaining powers of nature itself. We humans are the final interpreters of the religious, moral, aesthetic, and scientific meanings of nature, no matter whether our faith in all of these realms centers finally on nature or some other kind of religious or secularly assumed reality deemed to be more critically important than nature. But even in the second case, it is we who are the interpreters of that presumed other reality as being even more basic than nature.

To the extent that this faith recognizes and takes into serious account the *sacredness* of nature, whether inherently so or made such by some sort of nature-transcending power, to that extent I hold the faith to be *religious* (see Crosby 2022a: chapter 6). In any event, since we are the ones who have to do the interpreting, even of alleged religious authorities that are claimed to lie beyond our human comprehension to a significant extent, there is a basic sense in which the buck stops with us and our respective interpretations of what, if anything, is finally and most importantly and valuably real. Whatever it turns out to be, that is the focus of our faith, whether it be religious or secular. In any event, our indebtedness to, dependence on, and responsibility toward nature here on earth cannot be ignored. Our telic powers are in these manners brought forcibly and inevitably into play, and to refuse to make appropriate and much-needed use of them is folly of the highest order. What we do or refrain from doing has profound bearing on the fate of the earth.

Chapter 5 takes up the challenge of responding critically to an extended defense of *panpsychism* mounted by Mikael Leidenhag in a journal article and throughout a book devoted to this purpose. I take note of five of his basic arguments, presenting them as fairly and fully as I can, and then responding to each of them in turn—defending in this way my own *emergentist* account of teleology in contrast with his panpsychist position. His arguments are carefully thought out, and I try to do as much justice to their logic as I can while highlighting the counter logic of my own position. I am grateful that the different logics of the two positions can in this way be brought more clearly into light. Leidenhag is an able adversary and supports his position with admirable care and skill.

In the final section of this chapter, I discuss three types of theistic religion (traditional theism, pantheism, and panentheism). These types of theism give foundation to panpsychism, as Leidenhag notes, but he does not give explicit support of his own to any of the three. Assumed in each of the three is some kind of God, whether that God is thought to be the creator of the universe, pervasively present in it, or its being somehow present in God. God is typically assumed in each of the three religious perspectives to be a kind of being, presence, or power of a mental or spiritual order, meaning that psyche, spirit, or mind is primordial rather than derivative. This amounts, of course, to a kind of panpsychism.

I compare and contrast this kind of religious panpsychism with a discussion and defense of my own version of religious naturalism, in which psyche, mind, or spirit are emergent, not primordial phenomena, showing why for me nature is the most appropriate focus of religious commitment and why there is no need for appeal to God to account for psychic phenomena or to be the necessary focus of religious faith. I can respect and appreciate the appeal of the three kinds of theism Leidenhag makes note of, but I do not find them to be personally convincing.

Religion is a broad area of human thought and commitment, and there is ample room and even need for different versions of it, given the continuing debatability of even its greatest and most widely influential historical and contemporary versions. These many different versions expose the fallibility of human conceptuality and belief in the area of religion as in all other areas of thought and experience. Frank acknowledgment of this unavoidable human fallibility gives compelling evidence of the finally indescribable character, power, and greatness of the ultimate focus of each profound religious system. I celebrate and do not deplore this diversity, and Leidenhag's spirit, displayed in his writings, leads me to think that he would agree. So I take leave from him in this chapter on a charitable and pacific note. He is a partner in an extremely important philosophical enterprise.

Chapter 6 traces out the major stages in the evolution of mind and in this way offers further defense of an emergentist, non-eliminative (or nonreductive) account that requires no reference to any kind of preexisting psychic factor prior to the evolution of the earliest forms of life on earth. The key to the evolution of life, which counts as the earliest stage of the evolution of mind, is *organization*. This idea is the theme of the chapter. Increasing numbers of new types and levels of organization can be observed as we proceed from the matter-energy of the Big Bang origin of our present universe; to the evolution of ordinary atomic and molecular matter; to the evolution of living cells and systems of cells devoid of consciousness; to the evolution of conscious living ones; to the evolution of those with cultures of various types; and to the evolution of human beings and the great variety of their supporting and sustaining cultures that have developed and evolved in their histories on earth.

Throughout this process the roles of matter-energy and time are fundamental. Matter-energy provides the continual basis of these transformations, exhibiting a protean, extraordinarily alterable propensity throughout while still keeping its fundamental character. Time, with its combination of continuity and novelty, introduces changes and innovations that reach their highest levels of complexity—at least here on earth and in relation to psychic, teleological phenomena—with the emergence of human beings.

The clock of evolution cannot be set back because the novel or creative power of time brings into existence complexities of organization that were not there before. These evolving systems are genuinely and irreducibly new and can be observed even in the transition of the earliest kind of matter-energy in the Big Bang to the ordinary matter of atoms, molecules, microscopic systems, and macroscopic objects of various kinds. I conjecture that the Big Bang itself transforms ingredients of earlier complexes of world systems into the distinctive character of our present pluriverse.

The basic problem with the theory of panpsychism, in light of the continuing evolutionary process as I outline it in this chapter, is its strong tendency to overlook the creative role of time and of the protean character of matter-energy. Mind is an outcome of these two and not in any way a precondition for the presence of teleological phenomena on earth. And mind's emergence is a function of the complexity of organization. I illustrate this to be the case by the use of three analogies: the intricate organization of the bodies of living beings, a deck of cards, and democracy as a political system. No complex organization, no life, and no life, no mind.

The organization of the universe as I view it is not that of some kind of massive order that encompasses and contains all other orders. Instead, it is a multiplicity of orders of various types and sizes that includes many other orders, but no one of which contains all orders. And there is nothing existing that is not some sort of order. Hence, there are no simples, and there is no such thing as an order that contains all other orders. Every existing thing is a system of some sort, and there is no such thing as a master system said to contain all other systems. In making these crucial observations, I draw in the chapter on the thought of American philosophers Justus Buchler and Lawrence Cahoone.

These observations amount to the realization that the so-called *universe* is really a *pluriverse*. And it is a dynamic, fecund pluriverse of ongoing creation and destruction, relentless process and change. Outcomes of this dynamism on earth are, in their evolutionary sequences, ordinary matter, living matter, conscious living matter, and conscious living matter accompanied and assisted by various kinds of emergent culture, some relatively simple and others increasingly more complex. All of this is made possible by the *novel* aspect of time that is essential to time's flowing unidirectionally and irreversibly out of the past, through the present, and on into the future—and by the protean character of matter-energy endlessly amenable to ongoing transformation as it exhibits in itself the effects of the ever-gnawing tooth of time.

Why has time on earth continuously produced new orders of complexity of system and order? There is no answer to this "why" question other than that each formerly new emergent order has served as a kind of initial condition and impetus for the emergence of still newer, hitherto unprecedented orders. The universal "why" question thus admits of no clear, finally convincing answer. We can only say, fumblingly and inadequately, that it is in the nature of nature, as we have come to experience and know it, to operate in this way. We can explain aspects of natural order on the basis of other aspects, but we have no compelling requirement to try to explain the existence or most elemental properties and functions of nature itself. We can explain what is explainable by means of appeal to the givenness of nature, and we do not have to try to explain the existence of nature.

We are better equipped to answer the question of "how" nature has processed and evolved over eons, and I present an outline of what I take to be the principal stages of this process in chapter 6. There are marvel and miracle enough here so as not to require the positing of primordial teleology lying behind the universe conceived as a single-ordered whole and as imparting some kind of unitary, overarching purpose for life and mind on earth. Wholes within wholes, systems within systems, organizations within organizations, and no super-complex of all such, are overwhelming enough.

The endless fascination of the "how" does not require an underlying, all comprehending answer to the question of "why." Questions about purpose and not just ones about process can be meaningfully raised *within* the present pluriverse, not *about* it. Teleological phenomena, or goal-directed, purposive behavior—as I continue to theorize and emphasize throughout this book—is the outcome of immanent, gradually developing processes of material organization. There is no compelling need for it to be thought of as being already present and operative behind or inside these emerging processes.

The last part of chapter 6 provides an analysis of the psychological theory of behaviorism, showing it to be another example of the strong tendency to posit mind as something alien to matter and, as such, not amenable to scientific study in its own right. It is ironic that such a type of mind-body dualism should be assumed by some scientists as a way to insure the assumed objectivity or purely external character of scientific investigations and theories. Behaviorism can be seen in this way as another implausible kind of reductionism. As such, it fails to do justice to the fact that mental phenomena are genuinely real in their origination from and dependence on material bodies. In other words, minds are functions of bodies, but they cannot be reduced to earlier forms of those bodies. They are emergent realities and deserve to be studied and analyzed as such.

This point holds as true for mind as it does for life. Neither is some kind of mechanism but an aspect of reality that transcends the limits of mechanisms. Behaviorism is a tendency to look backward, not only to earlier stages in the evolution of matter but also to the Newtonian conception of matter as something inert and nonevolving. When viewed in that manner, mind comes naturally to be something that by its nature is radically immaterial and separate from matter. Implicit in this view is the idea that mind is not susceptible to scientific study, something that lies outside the domain of science.

Early modern philosophers resisted this idea, claiming that there can be something called science appropriate to the study of mind but focusing on a domain entirely distinct from matter. There would thus be two major kinds of science separate from one another and yet somehow also related to one another. This "somehow" was never resolved into a consistent, acceptable way of thinking. It either ended up with a final reduction of everything to the material, as *materialism,* or reduction of everything to the mental, as *idealism.*

Strongly resisting the idealist options, behaviorism chose materialism as an operational strategy. Mind can be studied scientifically, its proponents alleged, but only in terms of externally observable modes of physical behavior. Mind itself is basically only these modes and need not be thought of as something internal or phenomenological. Like all material phenomena, it is something mechanical or mechanistic. So far as science can discern, supposed interior qualities of mind and free actions of mind are reducible, in the final analysis, to externally accessible modes of motion, change, and behavior.

The method of scientific analysis can work only with externally and thus objectively observable phenomena, behaviorists reasoned, so mind becomes—at least for the purposes of scientific study—the study of behavior. A kind of reductive or eliminative materialism is thus assumed and proposed. The concept of matter this view assumes is basically the matter of Newtonian physics rather than the protean matter of biological evolution. Mind is nothing other in its true character than what is amenable to investigation by the field of physics. Material emergentism of the sort I have been describing in this chapter gives way, at least by strong implication, to reductionistic materialism. There is no real mentality in this outlook, and no purposive agency. Everything is reduced to external movements of the body. Whatever internal mental experiences or strivings there may be, these are negligible and unimportant to the extent that they cannot be reduced to scientifically observable behaviors of organisms, emphatically including the human ones.

As I point out toward the end of chapter 6, the philosopher Charles Taylor offers a convincing objection to the behavioristic way of thinking. He does so simply by observing that movements of the body such as two people shaking hands or dogs yelping and drooling over morsels of food held in someone's hand provide direct and unimpeachable evidence of their being intentional indications of both mentality and agency. They are not just external movements but reliable, everyday indicators of the reality of conscious minds and conscious agency. They give compelling indication of the evolution, in these two species of life, of purposive minds capable of initiating actions in the world.

It is therefore mentally intended *actions*, not mere mechanical *movements*, that their bodily behaviors reliably express and communicate. Minds are essential elements in any reasonable and reliable conception of reality. And they are essential without being in any way separate from their embodiments, their being actualities made possible by the evolution of matter and complex types of material organization capable of housing, supporting, and giving rise to the flourishing of irreducibly new and real mental phenomena of many different kinds.

Turning finally in this introduction to chapter 7, the last one of this book on teleology, I explore two options for religious faith and commitment: traditional Christian monotheism and my own stance of religious naturalism. I include this last chapter advisedly because I think that much of the appeal of panpsychism lies in its promise of providing primordial purpose, meaning, and value to human life. Its appeal is thus existential and not merely conceptual. As the fundamental part of this promise, it gives assurance of a personal God who has created the universe with a principal focus on human beings and with the fervent desire to enter into a loving relationship with them as fashioned in God's own image.

Prior to everything else, then, is the loving, saving, comforting presence and power of the putative God of the universe, and humans on earth are its principal beneficiaries. Not only that, but they are humble servants of God who are invited to live not only under God's protection but also constantly under God's judgment—a judgment essential to their flourishing as God's creatures. Notable in this monotheistic perspective is not only the idea that humans are created in the image of God, but also that God is in countless ways a radically anthropomorphic God whose humanlike traits are believed to be magnified to an infinite degree.

God is like us humans in many ways, and we are like God in many ways. A warm and reassuring relationship with God is therefore possible, despite the vast differences that also lie between our natures and the nature of God. God is both endlessly fascinating and saving while being at the same time awesomely daunting and powerful. God for monotheistic Christians is the personification of the sacred. God's sacredness pervades the universe, and it provides counsel, hope, support, judgment, and direction for every aspect of human life. God can also be seen as the impetus, direction, and guide for the evolutionary processes of the world when these are endorsed and accepted by Christians, making mind primordial rather than derivative, as in panpsychism. The allure of this vision of reality is undeniable. I acknowledge and respect it and those who are committed to it, but I do not assent to it.

My religious worldview is that of a religious naturalist for whom the irrepressible power and allure of the sacred resides in nature and not in something thought to be supernatural or surpassingly greater than nature. I find reassurance, purpose, and salvation in the immanence of nature itself with no felt need of recourse to some kind of being, presence, or power beyond nature. Nature is personable without being personal. We humans can be confidently at home here. We can humbly accept our status and role as conscious creatures of nature, with all of the gifts nature has conferred on us. We can cultivate a deep-lying sense of cooperation and community with the nonhuman types of life that are so prolific on the face of the earth. In doing so, we can gratefully acknowledge our dependency on the intricate ecological networks that make possible all kinds of life on earth, including our own. We can devote ourselves to nature's wellbeing on earth and to working for the preservation and flourishing of its millions of interdependent creatures in their respective domains.

We have abundant purpose, guidance, and *reason for being*, in our character as evolved creatures of nature. The sacred is solidly ensconced and operative in the material world and not elsewhere. Earth is our home, and we need ache, pine, or aspire toward no other. Like all the other creatures of nature, we come into being and eventually pass out of being. The only thing that is permanent and everlasting is nature itself, nature that extends even beyond this present universe (or, more properly, pluriverse) to all the others that have preceded and will follow it in endless time, and with endlessly evolving as well as devolving types of matter-energy. There is no need to puzzle in this magnificent view of reality about how a purely spiritual God, unlimited or unconstrained by any of the restrictions of temporal existence, can relate in intelligible ways to the fundamentally material and temporal character of nature. Moreover, anthropocentrism is not a nagging problem in religious naturalism's vision of the sacred. Nature is not a personal being.

This vision is inexhaustibly fascinating, mysterious, and sustaining in its own right, and is rich with deeply inspiring and motivating salvific power. Most fundamentally, at least for the purposes of this book, religious naturalism is not only content but delighted to regard mind, spirit, and purpose as emergent from the incredible fecundity and creativity of nature itself. I discuss themes, interrelations, and differences between traditional Christian theism and religious naturalism in chapter 7. In doing so, I have sought to give credible shape and form in this book to important aspects of my philosophical and religious interpretations of teleology, and to do so in the contexts of other related views. My focus throughout has been on the metaphysical and religious ultimacy of nature.

Nature may not have an external, overarching purpose, but it sings today on earth a resonant song of inspiration, challenge, and opportunity—but also of somber warning. Do we have the sensitivity and resolve to respond effectively to this song in our time of approaching ecological peril? Only time will tell. The song's drumbeat is quickening, sounding an ominous alarm that we must soon change some of the most deeply entrenched habits of our technological civilization. The opportune time for doing so may turn out to be shockingly short. Ours is a time of nature's judgment, laden with awesome responsibility. Nature can be a source of blissful assurance but also of rigorous demand—no less so for it than for the personal God of traditional monotheism.

Chapter One

Six Interpretations of Teleology

> If indeed existence precedes essence, one will never be able to explain one's action by reference to a given and specific human nature; in other words, there is no determinism—man is free; man *is* freedom. Nor, on the other hand, if God does not exist, are we provided with any values or commands that could legitimize our behavior. Thus we have neither behind us, nor before us in a luminous realm of values, any means of justification or excuse.
>
> —Jean-Paul Sartre (1948: 34)

In 1945, the French existentialist Jean-Paul Sartre presented a lecture, a version of which was published the following year under the title *L'existentialisme est un humanisme*. The preceding epigraph is quoted from an English translation of this work and captures its central theme. There is for Sartre no God, and there is no such thing as a fixed or determinate human nature. There are thus no such things as objective purposes or values, either conferred on human beings as part of the divine act of creating the world or implicit in a supposed common nature of all humankind. What account, then, does Sartre give of teleology?

Sartrean Teleology

For Sartre, "existence precedes essence," meaning that whatever nature human beings come to have over time is the cumulative effect of their acts of absolute freedom. In other words, humans create their natures over time, and do

23

so freely and without any kind of external standard, excuse, or constraint. They are therefore solely responsible for and only obligated to what they themselves create. Nothing is incumbent on any of them from the outset or from the outside. There are no antecedent values or commitments for which they are responsible. All values without exception are the subjective creations of their absolute, unrestrained freedom.

There is no option for humans of being anything other than totally responsible for their choices and actions. Their only antecedent "nature," if it be called that, is that humans are unrestrictedly free to define themselves as human beings. Each person inevitably does so, according to Sartre, by his or her freely chosen actions and contributes thereby to whatever humans have been, presently are, or will become. We humans have no nature or essence conferred on us from outside of ourselves. The only *teleology* or goal-directed thought and behavior anywhere in the world is what is posited and created de novo by each and every act of human freedom.

With humanity and only with humanity, according to Sartre, teleology or goal-directed choice and behavior come into the world. This teleology is ultimately arbitrary, without any sort of binding external purpose, guidance, or goal. Humans are entirely responsible for it. The world as such is devoid of purpose or value of any kind. There are no sheerly given, a priori, or divinely mandated moral or other kinds of principle on which human choices either can or ought to be based. Humans are abandoned and forlorn, left entirely to their own resources when it comes to issues of purpose and value. They must sheerly invent all of the meanings, ideals, and goals of their lives. Their entire status and value stem from their rootage in the awesome openness and absolute contingency of the decisions and actions of human beings.

Theistic Teleology

Sartre's philosophy represents one extreme end of an imagined spectrum when it comes to the question of whether teleology and an accompanying suite of moral and other kinds of meaning, value, and importance are somehow built into the universe as a whole. His answer to this question is a resounding "No." The universe has no purpose or goal, and there are no objective values.

At the other end of this spectrum is the idea that the world, and humans within the world, are responsible to valuative standards incorporated into it and levied on their species by God with the creation of the world. Thus the world as a whole and humans in the world have specific anteced- ent meanings, values, and purposes for their existence, a built-in, divinely endowed teleology. The creation of the world, its course, and the meaning of human life are guided, directed, and mandated by this divine teleology.

The polar opposite of the spectrum from Sartre's extreme conviction that centers solely on human choices and human responsibility for those choices is an equally extreme belief that the only real freedom in the universe is that of an *omnipotent* deity who predestines and controls every- thing that occurs in the world, including each and every human "choice" and action. In this extreme view, there are meanings, purposes, and values in the universe that transcend human choices. But the so-called human choices themselves are wholly expressions of God's continuing fiat, control, and power. The world is full of teleology or goal-directed and value-laden choices, but all of the choices are ultimately God's. Whatever purposes the world or humans have are God's purposes. Everything that occurs, without exception, has an explanation or reason, but all of these are finally God's, and many if not all of them are necessarily opaque to human imagination or understanding. This seems to be the lesson, for example, of the book of Job in the Hebrew Bible.

Critical Discussion of These Two Views of Teleology

These two extremes, that of Sartre's view that all goals and values in the universe stem from human choices without external guidance or norm, and traditional theism's conviction that objective values have their ultimate source in divine creation and rule over the world—whether with or without the existence of genuine human freedom—can help to frame our subsequent discussions of possible alternatives that fall between the extremes. I do not subscribe to either extreme. I am neither a Sartrean existentialist nor a convinced theist, to say nothing of being committed to the idea of divine omnipotence.

Furthermore, I do not endorse the idea that there is some sort of purpose for the existence *of* the world as such or as a whole, but I do strongly believe that there are ample meanings, purposes, and values present in and available to us *within* the world that can guide and are needed to guide our thoughts, choices, and actions as human beings. The latter have no transcendent, otherworldly source. They are wholly immanent in the world. But they do command our recognition, response, and fealty and do not arise solely from our arbitrary, unguided choices in a Sartrean manner. So if neither Sartrean existentialism nor traditional theism can explain the insistent reality of teleology and its place in our experiences of the world, what hypothesis can best serve this goal?

Even the raising of the question in this form, it should be noted, assumes that there is such a thing as teleology, at least in the sense of our having the end, goal, or purpose of seeking to resolve a fundamental philosophical question. To raise a question and to expect to find a meaningful and convincing answer to it are already to engage in teleological behavior. Implicit in my raising the question here is also to assume that the answer will not be merely one of arbitrary choice but one responsive to appropriate reasons, both pro and con, as a satisfactory answer is sought. Not just any "answer" plucked out of the blue will suffice.

And one is bound to raise the question of why it should be supposed that answers to questions about meaning, purpose, and value in human existence—philosophical, moral, aesthetic, religious, social, or cultural—should be any different. In other words, one has to presuppose the *intelligibility* of different aspects of the world, including the intelligibility of values in the world, if one is to raise questions about those aspects and to hope for meaningful answers to those questions. This fact in itself is a reminder of the importance of the question about the inescapable presence and undeniable roles of teleology in our ongoing interpretations and actions relating to ourselves and our lives in the world—the question that is the focus of this book.

The fact of purposes and aims in the world does not require that there be a purpose or aim of the world itself, as has often been commonly claimed and believed. But it does require us to seek a plausible account of why teleological purposes and aims are so prominent in our lives in the world. In my judgment, neither Sartre nor traditional theism supplies us with a satisfying account.

Sartre denies any kind of teleology other than the teleology of arbitrary choices, while traditional theism pushes the explanation entirely onto the will and purpose of a supposed creator of the world and everything in it. Traditional theism makes the source of teleology in the world ultimately the outcome of *God's* choices, in a manner similar to Sartre's insisting that the source is solely *human* choices. In both cases, we have a voluntarist rendering of standards for choice, which is to reason in a circle. The situation is similar to the familiar story of a mother who requests that her child do something. The child asks, "Why do I have to do it?" And the mother responds, "Because I *said* so!" In both cases, we leave hanging the critical issue of the distinction between choices themselves and the criticism and justification of choices.

Theistic voluntarism does not speak to this distinction unless we assume that God's choices are not arbitrary but reflect the responsible goodness and unimpeachable character of God's nature. Otherwise, whatever God chooses to do is by definition good, which seems like an arrested analysis of our question not only about the presence of teleology in the world but also about the norms and values needed for guidance and evaluation of our human goals and aims in the world. If God's choices are not responsible to or representative of anything other than themselves, then they are left without explanation or justification. Divine caprice is no substitute for unimpeachable divine goodness. Sartre, for his part, identifies values with normless choices, which hardly seems like an adequate analysis of the character and direction of responsible freedom. Taking responsibility for one's choices means more than acknowledging the fact of one's having made the choices. It also means acknowledging and accepting the obligation to justify to others as well as to oneself making the choices. "Just because I choose to do so" is not a pertinent or adequate justification either for humans or God.

Normless teleology such as that defended by Sartre may allow for the exercise of free choice or goal-directed behavior, but it provides no basis for a distinction between good and bad, rational and irrational, choices and behavior. An adequate teleology needs to take this distinction seriously into account. The mythical Satan, for example, may be radically free, but his radical freedom does not make him good. If anything, his normless freedom is precisely what makes him so destructive, malicious, and evil. He does what he pleases and wreaks havoc as a result. Similarly, a God possessed of Sartrean normless freedom permits no reliable prediction or expectation of God's always doing good and refraining from evil in relation to God's human creatures. A Sartrean God is a radically unreliable, undependable, untrustworthy God. Theists have sometimes defended the idea of such a God, but for the most part, traditional theists have proclaimed the dependable, saving goodness of God, a God defined at least to considerable extent by humanly recognizable and rationally defensible goodness and love.

One might humbly quake and submit in the presence of a God of normless freedom, never knowing what God might do next. But it is hard to know how one could love such a God or feel loved by such a God. Sartre does not believe in God, of course, but his conception of normless freedom, if it applies as he insists it does to all humans, leaves each person radically endangered by the free choices of others—especially the more powerful others—in a fashion similar to what would be their radically precarious and undependable relation to a normless God.

Neither divine nor human freedom is made automatically responsible, exemplary, or good simply by its arbitrary, normless exercise. In short, the question about teleology in the world and in the teleological choices of living beings in the world is closely connected with the question of the status and force of values and norms by which freedom can rightly be held responsible. The presence of teleology or goal-directed choice in us humans as part of the world presupposes the presence of emergent values in the world to which our choices can respond and on the basis of which we can find purpose, meaning, and fulfillment for the living of our lives.

The world as a whole may have no single purpose for its being, and I do not believe that it does. But it must somehow contain or make available knowable and dependable purposes and values in order for normative, as opposed to capricious, teleology within it to be possible. And what is true for us humans must also be true for other species of life in general, but especially for those life forms for which there is such a thing as conscious, goal-guided, value-centered choice. Consciousness and choice go necessarily together, as we shall see. And responsible choice requires objective, and not merely subjective, values—values discernible in their environments or particular worlds by beings able to make such choices.

Genuine freedom, if it exists, is a teleological phenomenon. Responsible freedom presupposes objective values to guide its choices. Discovery of truths in the world requires that truths as well as values have status and meaning independent of our choices—in other words, that these two aspects of the world can be made intelligible to us and, as such, incumbent on our beliefs and practices. I strongly believe that these two requirements are met in the world as we regularly experience it.

So far, I have briefly considered and rejected two theories relating to the question of teleology or goal-directed behavior, or behavior implicit in the search for objective truths and values and in choices and actions resulting from this search: Sartrean existentialism and traditional theism, especially but not only voluntarist theism. I now want critically to examine the cogency and convincingness of four other views, namely, eliminative, mechanistic materialism; the teleological panpsychism promoted by American philosopher Thomas Nagel; the bipolar metaphysics of Alfred North Whitehead; and an emergentist, indeterministic materialism. The last of these four constitutes my conception of teleology's most plausible, supportable character and significance. I offer reasons here and elsewhere in this book for regarding it as a better alternative than the three other views, and also better than the Sartrean and theistic ones already described and critically assessed.

Eliminative, Mechanistic Materialism

The type of materialism I describe and criticize in this section is *eliminative* because it claims that the whole of life, mind, and conscious mind can be *reduced* without remainder to the theories and laws of physics. It is *mechanistic* because it contends that these theories and laws describe a universe and everything in it that function, in the final analysis, in a wholly deterministic, predictable, and lawlike fashion. Whatever novelty there seems to be in it is not really that but only modes of functioning and behavior that cannot presently be reduced to, or as yet fully understood to be, in accord with strictly causal principles.

What seems to be a genuine inner life of qualitative conscious awareness is only an epiphenomenon or illusory play of seeming qualities, and what might seem to be freedom of response and action is not really that but only behavior that accords completely with causal determinism. Teleology, if it be called that, is a mechanical mode of behavior with no hint of could-have-done-otherwise (the causal conditions remaining the same) activity involved. This interpretation of the nature of freedom is called *compatibilism*. It claims that freedom and determinism are entirely compatible, the term *freedom* designating only those choices and actions stemming from within a person, as contrasted with those imposed on the person by some kinds of external source and constraint. So long as the nexus of causes explaining my action arises at least penultimately from within me, the action is said to be free. This is said to be so even though the nexus itself is nothing more than a congeries of causes that stems ultimately from the mechanics of my physical makeup as my mechanical nature interacts with a mechanical, deterministic world—everything in the world claimed to be exhaustively explicable by the theories and principles of a wholly mathematical, deductive, causally controlled physics.

In such a physics, everything that exists is material, and all material functioning is mechanical. Issues of purpose, meaning, and value that might be assumed to lie beyond the competence or reach of physics, whether in fact or in principle, are rejected as ultimately unreal. Biology, for example, is simply a subset of physics, all of its principles and explanations reducible to those of physics. It is not a *complement* to physics but only one *version* of physics. The same is true of psychology and of all other subjects of thought and inquiry in the world.

What may look like goal-directed behavior or *teleology* in that sense of the term is rejected in favor of the conviction that everything that occurs, including all things living and all human culture, choice, and behavior, is attributable to antecedent, wholly constraining causes. There is no such thing as real chance or genuine novelty anywhere in the world, including in the processes of biological evolution through millions of years. Everything that happens does so in strict accord with universal causal and mathematical predictability and certainty. Baruch Spinoza in the seventeenth century and Albert Einstein in the twentieth were famous champions of this conception of reality. It is highly significant that both of them, in doing so, were led to deny the ultimate reality of *time*, a consequence of causal determinism and insistence on mathematical certainty in reasoning about the universe I shall discuss later in this chapter.

Humans in particular are nothing more than robots in the perspective of eliminative materialism, a statement that is equally true of all other kinds of life. Paradoxically, this view has to encompass even the scientists who have arrived at and currently propound the theory of eliminative materialism, leaving no room for a distinction between a *caused* physical theory, proposition, or belief and a *justified* one, to say nothing of a causally determined choice and a genuinely free one made in the presence of actually accessible different courses of possible thought, choice, and action. Causation and rational persuasion have become indistinguishable.

The eliminative materialist philosopher Daniel C. Dennett brushes aside the criticism that his view consigns humans to the status of robotic machines and thereby makes this view radically implausible. He contends that experienced "qualia" can be "replaced by dispositional states of the brain" and that the human "self" can easily be conceived as "a valuable abstraction, a theorist's fiction rather than an internal observer or boss" (1991: 431). He goes on readily to admit that it is "mind-bogglingly difficult to imagine how the computer brain of a robot could support consciousness" but that it is no less difficult "to imagine how an organic human brain" could do so. "How," he asks, "could a complicated slew of electrochemical interactions between billions of neurons amount to conscious experiences? And yet we readily imagine human beings to be conscious, even if we still can't imagine how this could be" (1991: 433).

I have three responses to this reasoning. The first is that I do not doubt that the mind is a function of the body. I, like Dennett, am a materialist, but mine is an emergentist materialism, as I shall explain in a later section of this chapter, not the reductive or eliminative kind of materialist he defends. My second response is that the robotic simulacrum of a conscious human being he imagines does not currently exist and that if it were someday to be created, it would be the product of ingenious human intention and design, compelling evidence of the intentional, teleological, end-oriented, end-directed freedom Dennett purports to refute. Third, our creation of the conscious robot, if that were possible, would only be a *replication* of the mind-body problem rather than a *solution* to it if there continued to be considerable unclarity about how such material structures and functions should prove able to produce firsthand mental phenomena. Current computer technology gives us no convincing evidence of how this could be possible. We already know *that* material bodies can produce and support minds, but we are not at all sure *how* they do so.

Dennett treats freedom in similar eliminative fashion, arguing that while it is true for him that everything in the world is causally determined, we humans "have evolved to be entities *designed* to change their natures in response to their interactions with the rest of the world." We do so in a manner similar to that of computers that make use of generators of diversity. The "randomness" of such generators need not be regarded "as truly random in the sense of indeterminism." In a similar vein, he argues that although the future may be fixed, as he firmly believes it to be, this "God's eye" perspective is different from "the engaged perspective of an agent *within* the universe" where the universe appears to be open rather than causally determined (2004: 93). Randomness, Dennett insists, is only in the eye of the human beholder and has for him no metaphysical reality. All so-called chance is just ignorance of underlying causal factors that, if known and taken fully into account, would provide a complete explanation of any phenomenon, whether mental or physical.

The same conclusion would hold true for teleology in general, if we mean by it the possibility of some truly open-ended, principle-guided thought and behavior opted for in the face of a future that is not fixed in advance but has different realizable alternatives for change and development at given times. Dennett strongly rejects teleology in this sense. But his random generators are not the same thing as acts of intentional freedom, nor is it at all clear from his discussion how they could produce such acts or our routine apparent experiences of them. Finally, causal determinism is the main theory at issue in my discussion here, and its truth cannot simply be assumed as being a necessary part of an adequate interpretation of intentional, goal-directed, teleological freedom. For reasons such as the ones I have presented in this section, I do not regard eliminative, deterministic explanations of teleology to be convincing.

In sum, eliminative materialism explains teleology by explaining it away. I submit that it even explains away its own intentional proponents and reasoners. Physics is only a part, albeit an essential one, of the story that needs to be told about teleology and many other topics. Eliminative materialism is but one interpretation of the character, scope, and competency of physics, and is at bottom a self-stultifying one at that. It provides no satisfying explanation for teleology or convincing interpretation of its critical role in all life forms and especially in the lives of human beings, including the life and work of physicists themselves.

Causality is undeniably important and real. It has a fundamental role to play in physics and all other lines of inquiry. But if indeterministic teleology is also real, as I strongly believe and will continue to argue it to be, then the claimed all-encompassing, all-controlling character of causal determinism and the conviction of the ultimate, in-principle mathematical character and deductive certainty of everything in the world must be rejected—and with it, the credibility of eliminative materialism as a way of interpreting and finally discounting teleological phenomena of any kind, or at least of any kind that does not fit snugly within this too constricting mold.

Thomas Nagel's Panpsychist Teleology

Thomas Nagel argues that teleology has to be a primordial, underived, always present feature of the universe if its pervasive presence in the world as experienced by human beings is adequately to be explained. Teleological modes of behavior and the norms pertaining to and implicit within it do not for him emerge through biological evolution over a long passage of time but rather precede, underlie, and guide biological evolution as the essential precondition of its every stage—as fundamental a condition as other seeming preconditions such as matter, space, or time.

The fact of pervasive end-directed thought and action in human life gives convincing evidence to Nagel of teleology's primordial status and importance, an importance that pertains to all living creatures in the world and to the discovery of valuative standards implicit in our experiences of the world that are appropriate and needed to guide our beliefs, commitments, and behaviors. He is convinced that the bedrock character of teleological phenomena—as exhibited in what he takes to be some kind of guidedness and directedness in biological evolution as well as in human experiences and in the experiences of other animals—requires that we accord to the world as a whole a kind of panpsychical or mentalistic aspect, as supplemental to its physical, causal, and temporal aspects.

Ours is a teleological world from its origins to the present; hence, teleology is primordial rather than derivative from something more fundamental. It does not emerge. It has always been an essential trait of the world. The evolution of life and mind on earth testify to its preexistent, underived character. They do not give rise to it. They presuppose it, according to Nagel. Similarly, the values needed to guide telic modes of behavior are also implicit in the environments of creatures possessed of life and of some form of mind, however primitive and unsophisticated the latter may be in particular kinds of life. And for Nagel, even the intelligibility of features of the earth and of life on earth gives evidence of a pervasive teleology that invites investigation and response from creatures having at least some modicum of rational, goal-oriented, adaptive behavior.

The philosopher Evan Thompson does not defend a primordial teleology, but he does argue extensively in his book *Mind in Life* that all of the evolved life forms on earth have the three basic traits of *mind*, namely, autopoiesis (self-making and self-maintaining), sentience (sense making or feeling for the opportunities and demands of an organism's environment), and purposiveness (ability to function effectively and tend to its needs in its environment, and to do so with some degree of freedom and recognition of value). These three traits of life give evidence to Thompson of an "intrinsic teleology" or "immanent purposiveness" in all of life, from the most elementary forms of it to the most highly developed ones (Thompson 2007: 148, 152–54). Early life forms are thus by their very nature goal-oriented, goal-seeking creatures, and the evolutionary precursors of those with consciously intended teleological capabilities.

But Nagel is not satisfied, as Thompson is, with an evolutionary account of how teleology comes into the world. He is convinced that some kind of immanent teleological factor, force, impulse, or set of "natural teleological laws" (Nagel 2012: 66) must be operative—along with its efficient causal ones—within nature from the very beginning, laws that permit life on earth, with its teleological tendencies, capacities, adaptive abilities, and implicit values to evolve. He summarizes his view toward the end of his book when he explains that

> even though natural selection partly determines the details of the forms of life and consciousness that exist, and the relations among them, the existence of the genetic material and the possible forms it makes available for selection have to be explained in some other way. The teleological hypothesis is that these things can be determined not merely by value-free chemistry and physics but also by something else, namely, a cosmic predisposition to the formation of life, consciousness, and the value that is inseparable from them. (123)

He goes on to insist that "no viable account, even a purely speculative one, seems to be available of how a system as staggeringly functionally complex and information rich as a self-reproducing cell, controlled by DNA, RNA, or some predecessor, could have arisen by chemical evolution alone from a dead environment" (123).

Nagel's view of life, like that of Charles Darwin, Evan Thompson, many contemporary scientists and philosophers, and my own, is avowedly emergentist and nonreductive. But in contrast with these views, he does not regard *teleology* as something that emerges. Rather, he sees it as a presupposed, primordial, underived principle or impetus that makes emergence of all life, purpose, meaning, and value possible. Teleology underlies and guides evolution rather than being created by it.

Evolution has palpable direction and is guided in its ongoing developments by immanent ends or cosmic goals. Only in this way, Nagel is convinced, can we provide an adequate explanation of the pervasive presence on earth of teleological purposes, values, and modes of organic, goal-directed behavior. In this manner, he is led by this reasoning to posit the thesis that reality must be characterized as having a fundamental psychic aspect, as being panpsychical or psychophysical in its elemental nature (57–58, 61–63, 87). Mindless matter will not suffice as the source of a supposedly emergentist teleology. Both reductionist and emergentist materialism must be rejected.

I take issue with Nagel's interpretation of teleology in the seventh section. In it I also defend an emergentist, indeterminist alternative to the eliminative, mechanistic (or causally determinist), and materialistic interpretation of it proffered by Daniel Dennett and others. In doing so, I also endorse a type of materialistic metaphysics that is entirely consistent with a robust teleology.

Whitehead's Bipolar Metaphysics

Insightful interpreter and exponent of the metaphysics of Alfred North Whitehead David E. Conner argues that some kind of mentalism or mental factor must be primordial if matter-energy is first to generate over evolutionary time teleological living beings and then ones with emerging degrees of conscious mentality. Conner interprets Whitehead's "bipolar" or physical-mental actual entities (Whitehead 1975: 108–09) as ones that at the outset necessarily complement their *physical* aspect with a *mental* one of "the ability to assess information at some utterly simple level" (2019: 213). Without recognition of this rudimentary mental capacity, Conner argues, evolutionary emergentism could not occur.

I believe, in contrast, that the ongoing passage of primordial time can make enormous changes in equally primordial and amazingly protean matter-energy, by virtue of time's own essential character as combining continuity with novelty. The role of Whitehead's *Creativity* as the putative "Category of the Ultimate" (Whitehead 1975: 21–22) is in my metaphysical outlook played by the creative (as well as the necessarily destructive) power of *primordial time* working—with neither ultimate beginning nor ultimate ending—on *primordial matter-energy*. In order for something new to come into being, something old must be left behind, meaning that the past thereby becomes fixed and unrepeatable in itself. But the old is not then entirely lost but transformed into and carried in that manner into the new. There is no such thing as spontaneous generation of anything, no de novo change. All change is *transformation* of something already in existence, and this fact can clearly be seen in the histories of cosmic, terrestrial, and biological evolution, as well as in all kinds of cultural change.

The relationship between the two primordials I have identified is what lies behind emergent evolution and what gives rise to life and rudimentary mind. Mind is therefore *emergent*, not primordial, in contrast with Whitehead's bipolar theory. Mind makes its first telic appearance, as I pointed out in the introduction, in the self-making and self-maintaining of organisms or forms of life as they interact agentially with their environments by taking account of possibilities and requirements for flourishing and survival offered by those environments. This is the first emergence of purposive beings,

beings equipped to alter and respond as purposive, goal-seeking agents to the possibilities and constraints of their environmental settings. *Conscious* mentality, purposiveness, and creation of cultures of various times come later in the evolutionary process, as I shall now proceed to argue in more detail.

Emergentist, Indeterminist, Materialist Teleology

My metaphysical outlook is based on two primordial principles: matter-energy and time. Matter-energy is what persists through all temporal change, and all types of change exhibit the primordial character of time. Thus innumerable kinds of material realities, living and nonliving, living and conscious, and living and nonconscious, have come into existence on earth over the passage of time from its earliest stages of development to its present stage. Matter-energy is extremely protean and processive and thus amenable to these evolutionary transformations.

Primordial time, for its part, is indeterministic in its fundamental nature. It exhibits not only continuity in its passage but also ineliminable novelty, even if it be only the newness of its present moments, in contrast with its past ones. Their presentness is their newness, even if only the newness of replication—or, more accurately, near replication—of past moments. In other words, without novelty or newness there would be no such thing as the flow of time. But over stretches of time, and especially over vast stretches of it, astoundingly novel realities can come into being.

Thus time gives rise to emerging new possibilities, and these possibilities, in their turn, can become new actualities. There are in my metaphysics no such things as the *pure* predicables or *pure* possibilities posited by philosophers like Plato and Alfred North Whitehead. These exist only in imagination. All possibilities in temporal changes without exception are *real* ones, that is, possibilities posed by past actualities. Emergence builds on past actualities and combinations and systems of such that serve as real possibilities capable of being transformed into new actualities. The latter can then function as the basis and impetus for the continuing emergence of still different actualities.

There is thus a fundamental kind of creativity in all of nature, but we should also remind ourselves that this creativity is made possible by some amount of destruction. At the very minimum, the past must be left behind in order that the present can emerge. And sometimes the destruction of much in the past is required for new things to emerge, survive, and thrive.

A familiar example of this fact on an earthwide scale is the extinction of most of the dinosaurs sixty-five million years ago that made possible most of the mammalian life on earth today. Examples closer to home are those of routine animal predations, including the earthwide predations of other animals by humans, and the inevitable deaths of all biological organisms, including the mortal span of each human life.

One of the new kinds of reality emergent from the real possibilities posed for transformation by earlier forms of reality is the emergence of life itself, with the three traits of life and mind described by Evan Thompson. These three traits are teleological modes of adaptation to the environments of life forms that develop and are sustained by the essential adaptive capabilities the traits confer on these life forms. Conscious mind and sophisticated teleological thought, imagination, and intention develop evolutionarily and do so initially and principally because of their great adaptive utility. Factors such as sexual selection, chance mutations, genetic drift, and changing environments conspire to produce new forms of life, and some of the new populations of emergent life are more fit to survive in particular environments than others are. Life itself is generally believed today to be an emergent phenomenon on earth, but exactly when, where, and how it emerged is not fully understood or agreed upon.

With the development of degrees of consciousness inevitably goes the development of degrees of intentional freedom of thought and action. It does so because consciousness would have little adaptive utility or purpose without the freedom to put its feelings, deliberations, and other modes of awareness into practice. Unconscious reflexive responses have an important role to play in the life of an organism, but consciousness greatly expands the range of responses and actions available to it. Values are implicit in such adaptations, and with ongoing evolution they become more conscious, explicit, and appreciated for their own sake. Rationality also emerges and becomes a telic function for its own sake and for the sake of the appropriate actions it helps to make possible. And with consciousness, rationality, and awareness of value, intentional freedom comes increasingly to the fore. Philosophy, science, moral and legal systems, art, culture, and the like are fruits of this process and are greatly assisted by the origin and development of human language—as emergent, new real possibilities permit emergent actualities to be brought into being.

The upshot of all of the aforementioned is that teleology emerges on earth with the purposiveness or goal directedness of all forms of life, and with the evolution of new real possibilities that are capable of becoming new actualities, especially with the guidance of kinds and degrees of conscious awareness. It does so in my view through the interactions of two and only two primordial actualities, namely matter-energy and time. Continuing transformations of the first of these two primordial realities by persistent temporal changes are the continuing sources of new real possibilities that can become new material actualities—nonliving and living, unconscious and conscious, over enormous stretches of time.

Included in the lives of conscious animals are *imagined possibilities* sufficiently related to or associated with real ones that they can be made into actualities by performances of thought and will, the latter two still being functions of the physical characters of living beings and capable of being expressed and enshrined by humans in such physical media as gestures, spoken or written language, artistic creations, inscribed and communicable theoretical formulas, legal documents, or works of technical craft and manufacture. Possibilities can also remain as purely imagined, but in that case they are not—or not as yet—converted into something extramental and remain functions of the consciousness of human or nonhuman animals who envision and entertain them.

And yet, they are *real* if they can be shown to be *realizable* in something more than the individual minds of those who conceive them. Thus, for example, steam engines, locomotives, motorized ferry boats, airliners, and spaceships were first imagined and then the imaginary ideals became, with their further conceptual development, real possibilities that were finally converted into actualities. The same has been true of great works of religion, the arts, philosophy, politics, and the sciences, originating first as possibilities in the minds of creative thinkers.

No transcendent, otherworldly source of such possibilities is required. Minds are by their nature sources of imagined possibilities, most of them responding in various ways to earlier feats of imagination by others. And all of them, if capable of becoming actualities, are such by virtue of the character of nature at particular times—and ultimately by matter-energy continually given its dynamic, ever-changing character through the ages by the reality of time.

Such imaginable possibilities are located in this sense in nature as it continues to develop and emerge, and not in some kind of nonnatural, immaterial realm. The fact that no antecedent realm of pure possibility is required helps to explain why nothing ultimately immaterial, such as some kind of immaterial teleology or purely mental or spiritual purpose or set of purposes for the world as a whole is required. Matter-energy and time provide all the possibility needed, and this wealth of real possibility is located in these two primordial realities. And all of the explanations, purposes, values, and meanings required are natural, not extra-natural or supernatural. The natural is all that there is, but its prolific riches and possibilities lie beyond the reach or adequate expression of even the most fecund imaginations.

The newer stages of evolutionary emergence cannot be reduced to the earlier stages because they are unprecedented in varying degrees and always to that extent are genuinely new. Determinism, by insisting that efficient causes are in the final analysis both necessary and sufficient to account for their effects and for whatever occurs, fails to allow even for an intelligible distinction between causes and their effects. Effects are by this reckoning entirely reducible to their causes and thus not really different from their causes. Time and all temporal change collapse into something ontologically static and unchanging, and the distinction between antecedent causes and their subsequent effects that is so crucial to causal determinism goes by the board.

Cause-effect relations, like all temporal ones in general, exhibit the inseparable characters of both continuity and novelty, and do so in varying degrees. To dismiss genuine novelty from the natural world would be to deny its essential dependence on time and to reject the historical emergence of its present traits that include the teleological functions, strivings, adaptations, and purposive behaviors of all forms of life, and especially of its most complex and sophisticated forms. Purposive strivings would lose all meaning in the absence of time, and there would be nothing capable of such strivings in the absence of multiple forms of matter-energy that exhibit the three essential traits of every kind of life.

Conclusion

Tradition tells us that the Protestant reformer Martin Luther tacked ninety-five theses at the entrance to the Castle Church at Wittenberg in order to protest and pose for debate certain teachings of the Roman Catholic Church in his time. He did prepare such theses but probably did not do something so dramatic as tacking them on the church entrance. I shall conclude this first chapter by listing in fifteen points the central claims of the chapter. These points not only summarize the main theses of the chapter. They also point ahead to the chapters that will follow by providing the basis for what will be claimed and argued for in these subsequent chapters.

Here, then, are my fifteen points. I list them as a summary of what the present chapter asserts and defends.

1. No overarching, all-encompassing teleology or guiding purpose of nature itself either exists or is required.

2. No creator God is needed to account for nature's ongoing emergent creativity.

3. No transcendent realm of pure possibility is needed. All possibilities are real possibilities.

4. Matter-energy and time are the only primordial realities.

5. Meanings, purposes, values, telic phenomena of all kinds, life, and consciousness itself—all of these are emergent, not primordial.

6. Teleology comes into the world with the evolution of life.

7. The ongoing transformations of matter-energy are made possible by time.

8. Such transformations necessarily involve novelty, contingency, or chance, not mere continuity.

9. Causal determinism is therefore false.

10. Emergentism is opposed to reductionist or eliminative materialism. The flow of time is irreversible; its later stages cannot be reduced to its earlier ones. Genuinely new things occur with the flow of time.

11. Consciousness and freedom are inseparable. The former would have had no evolutionary, adaptive use without the latter.

12. Causal determinism and freedom are contradictory, not compatible.

13. Without God, nature is replete with purposes and purposive beings, even though it has no final, more ultimate purpose, reason, or explanation for its own being.

14. These immanent purposes and their attendant values provide more than enough of what is needed for flourishing and

meaningful human life, and for guiding purposeful human choices.

15. The basis for all purpose and explanation is nature, not something prior to or more fundamental than nature.

These theses are admittedly debatable, and some of them are no doubt highly debatable for those who think differently. I will continue to emphasize and defend their plausibility, coherence, and truth in the discussions ahead as I develop important supplemental approaches, claims, and applications— all of them relating in various ways to this book's fundamental focus on teleological issues, outlooks, and practices of various kinds.

Chapter Two

Two Meanings of *Telos*

Whenever there is plainly some final end, to which a motion tends should nothing stand in the way, we always say that such [a] final end is the aim or purpose of the motion, and from this it is evident that there must be a something or other really existing, corresponding to what we call by the name of Nature.

—Aristotle (1941a, I, 1: 24ff., 649)

There are two interpretations of the Greek word *telos* that we need constantly to bear in mind and distinguish as we continue to reflect on the topic of teleology that was introduced in the previous chapter. This word has frequently been translated into English as "purpose" and is translated in this way in the preceding epigraph taken from Aristotle's work *On the Parts of Animals*. But in Aristotle's philosophy, which has inspired much of the discussion and application of the term *telos* historically, the term does not fundamentally mean "purpose" in the sense that Aristotle believed there to be some kind of conscious purpose or intended goal implicit in or required to explain all of nature. There is purposive behavior or intentional thought and action for Aristotle only in the case of human beings, exhibiting what for him are their unique, inimitable rational and volitional capabilities.

I argued in the previous chapter that teleology is exhibited not only in humans, but in all forms of life as such, in the sense that all forms of life exhibit adaptive behaviors of some sort as they relate to one another and to situations, opportunities, threats, and demands of their natural environments. But this behavior becomes *intentionally purposive* only with the

43

evolution of *conscious* beings—the beings with consciousness of various sorts and degrees that include many other kinds of life than the human one. In short, then, nature itself has no purpose of any kind, including some kind of *divinely bestowed* overall purpose for its existence. Nature as I regard it is the nonpurposive source from which purposive life forms emerge.

But what about Aristotle's so-called Unmoved Mover, depicted and argued for in his work *Physics*? Is not all of nature for him oriented toward this end as its overriding purpose? In my interpretation of Aristotle's thought, the Unmoved Mover is simply the essential form, actuality, or complete reality (*entelecheia*) of nature as a whole. All of the aspects of nature act in a coordinated, interconnected fashion to exhibit this form of the whole, which is Aristotle's way of characterizing nature as a system that functions in an orderly, predictable, and unitary fashion. The Unmoved Mover has no intentional purpose either in itself or one that it bestows on the whole of nature (*phusis*). The general character that nature's wholistic functioning exhibits is "teleological" only in its having this systematic aspect. Nature subserves the *telos* or end of its regular, orderly, predictable processes (Aristotle 1941b, VIII: 6, 260ff., 376–77).

What is for Aristotle true of nature as a whole is also true of its biological aspects. These too function for the most part in regular, orderly, predictable ways. Their processes or changes can be understood in terms of their *telē*, meaning in this context their characteristic developments over their ordinary life spans from their births to their deaths. These processes are teleological *only* in this restricted sense, not in the sense of having some kind of externally imposed purpose or divinely endowed reason for being. A teleology of consciously envisioned purposes is something altogether different for Aristotle. He is sympathetic with the idea that consciously intended ends are important capabilities of humans that reflect their definitive natures as rational beings. Humans can rightly be said to be *purposive* beings in this sense. But he does not extend this kind of teleology to the whole of nature.

Nature as a whole has a unitary, orderly, all-encompassing *telos* for Aristotle, but this term does not connote for him some kind of directive or guiding *purpose*. The translation of *telos* as "aim" or "purpose" in the epigraph to this chapter is therefore incorrect. As the historian of Western philosophy John Herman Randall Jr. points out, the term *purpose* in English typically means "foresight" and "intention" but this is not what Aristotle has in mind when he speaks of the *telē* of nonhuman animals or the *telos* of the whole of nature (Randall 1960: 125). It only means in these two contexts something like usual, repeated, or expected outcomes with regular stages of development that culminate in these outcomes or *telē*.

This crucial distinction having been drawn, there is something indispensably relevant for the present chapter in Aristotle's idea of nonpurposive ends or regularities of function as we continue in this chapter to think about the topic of teleology. While, as I persist in arguing, nature has no purpose for its being, it does exhibit a pervasive trait that is extremely important for my aim in writing this book. This trait is the observable movement in nature, at least to the extent that we can understand nature today, from relative simplicity and absence of living order toward ever-increasing structural complexity and order.[1] Aristotle has no conception of this movement. His conception of nature is devoid of evolutionary change. But the movement is notably and unavoidably discernible for us from the Big Bang origin of the present universe, as that is conceived in physics today, to its present extremely complex structures, including the structures of animal bodies and especially of animal nervous systems and brains.

Moreover, as outcomes of this ongoing process of change and development, nature on earth has given rise to countless kinds of living animals with their immanent trait of "purposiveness," as Evan Thompson calls it, as well as to the conscious purposiveness, involving foresight and intention, of a significant number of these living animals, including us humans. In other words, many nonhuman animals, like human ones, have some kind of consciously felt aim and goal-directed awareness in their relations to their natural environments, in consequence of their having some degree of consciousness.

But all living creatures, conscious or not, exhibit *telē* in the first, much broader, sense of the term as Aristotle uses it, namely, that of having regular, predictable, characteristic courses of change and development, action and reaction, from birth, to maturation, to old age, and to their eventual deaths. The two usages should not be confused. But we should note that this first one, over time, makes the second one at first possible and then actual. Emergentism exhibits both of these meanings of *telos*. First there is the origin of life itself from nonlife, in relatively primitive forms, then the natural emergence of many different and increasingly sophisticated kinds of life with their nonconscious, environmentally adaptive forms of behavior that can be called purposive or goal directed *only in this sense*. But much later on, conditions come into being that make possible life forms with *consciously intended* purposes.

How does this last observation relate to teleology, the theme of this book? It means that there is a seemingly relentless drive in nature on earth as we observe, interpret, and understand it today to produce life forms with their immanent "purposiveness" or *unconscious* adaptive behaviors[2] and then, later on, conscious beings with consciously envisioned and intended *telē*. This process does not mean that nature has somehow been *intended* from the start to do so or that it either has or has been given the *purpose* of doing so. It means only that it is in the nature of nature—its self-contained, self-sufficient character of being what it is—to do so. It means nature is "doing its thing," at least on earth, as we have currently come to understand how or by what sequential processes its potentialities emerge and become actual.

Thus, purposes of many kinds have arisen from the womb of nature, but nature itself has no antecedent or underlying purpose, no immanent or transcendent kind of goal-oriented, goal-tending, or goal-realizing end. Nature is undeniably orderly, regular, and predictable in many of its aspects. And it has an undeniably creative capacity, as exhibited by its phases of development on earth and elsewhere in the emerging cosmos, from the conjectured Big Bang to the present. Here as always, what for me does the ultimate explaining is not something beyond, outside, or independent of nature but nature itself. Nature produces teleology but is not produced by it.

Nature on earth has produced teleological beings in the forms of its millions of species of life, but it is not itself the product or expression of some kind of primordial, original teleological principle, impetus, or power. Teleology has gradually become a part of nature, but it has not always been there. It is an outcome of the unceasing interactions of the two primordials, matter-energy and time. *Emergentism* is a good substitute term for the *nonintentional sense* of Aristotle's term *telos*. By its processes and means, the unconscious, unintentional, adaptive sense of the term *purpose* as exhibited in all of life and then its consciously intentional sense in increasingly conscious forms of life are progressively embodied, enlivened, and brought into being. In stark contrast with Aristotle's static nature, nature as we conceive it today is dynamic. Out of its creative dynamism conscious purposes come into being. None is operative or immanent from the outset.

New possibilities continuously emerge and, on their basis, new actualities. And these new actualities include beings capable of consciously entertaining and acting upon the envisioned possibilities of their active minds. In my view of things, as well as in the view of the natural sciences today, Thomas Nagel's conviction in his book *Mind and Cosmos* that some kind of primordial teleological principle is required to account for the evolution of life on earth, the adaptive functions of life, and conscious purposiveness among humans and other conscious kinds of life need not be imagined or presupposed. The "hows" of nature's processes precede its "whys," the second coming into being by the agency of the first. Nagel puts the cart before the horse.

I want now to take a brief look at these natural "hows," as we understand or at least partially understand them today, just to illustrate how wonderous and complex the creative structures, functions, and operations of nature are that have made possible the evolution of life, the many forms of life possessed of some degrees of consciousness, and our own comparatively high level of consciousness, as creatures of nature. In the next three sections, I shall first focus briefly on the emergence of life itself; in the second one, on the equally astounding marvel of the many kinds of conscious life; and in the third one on the physical conditions that underlie and make possible human consciousness. There is much about these three topics that we do not presently comprehend, but there is also much that we have come to understand about them. A reasonable assessment and understanding of the topic of teleology, the central concern of this book, is critically dependent on each of them. Together, they suffice to show that teleology is emergent, not primordial, and that matter-energy and time can be seen as their two primordial bases.

Preconditions of Life

When I speak of matter-energy and time as *primordial* I mean to assert that neither of them is the outcome of, produced by, or created by something else. They both always have and always will exist. Furthermore, neither of them is made of something more fundamental than itself, and together they are the primal sources of all that has or ever will exist.

Thus, time is not created by motion or change; rates of motion or change are commonly and practically used as measurements of time, but they are not the same thing as time. Similarly, it makes no sense to ask, "What is matter-energy made of?" because everything else that emerges and comes into being over endless time is made of it. Our only way of understanding it is to recognize it as primordial and to interpret its character in terms of everything that it has shown itself to be capable of producing and becoming. Not even the supposed Big Bang is primordial in my view. Neither matter-energy nor time is brought into being by its agency. Instead, the two of them bring everything that has existed or ever will exist into reality, including the Big Bang.

The matter-energy of our present universe or face of nature has produced, in its interactions with time and by means of the Big Bang, both ordinary matter—the matter of objects on earth and in distant space that can be detected and studied with electromagnetic waves, including those of light—and so-called dark matter, the matter that does not reflect these kinds of wave. It has produced ordinary energy and so-called dark energy, the energy expressed in the cosmological constant that accounts for the accelerating expansion of our universe of galaxies and stars. According to our current science, dark matter and dark energy comprise about 95 percent of our present universe. Primordial matter-energy has also produced the four fundamental forces: gravitation, electromagnetic force, the strong force that holds the nuclei of atoms together, and the weak force that is responsible for the radioactive decay of atoms.

Emergent from matter-energy over large spans of time are various sorts of atoms, beginning with the hydrogen atom, with its one electron and one nucleic proton but soon expanding into a wide array of atoms, each with its particular atomic weight and distinctive number of electrons, protons, and neutrons (only hydrogen lacks neutrons). These atoms are capable of bonding with other atoms, in this way producing molecules of many different kinds. Combinations of molecules constitute the physical features of our customary world.

Evolution of Life

You and I are complexes of such atoms and molecules, and they make possible all that we are capable of thinking and doing. In particular, they make possible our teleological modes of reflecting, reasoning, and acting. Such combinations also constitute the origins and actions of every kind of life on the face of the earth. These too are teleological beings, whether they are conscious or unconscious, because of the purposiveness or end directedness of their adaptive behaviors in relation to their natural environments. Even the simplest bacterium has to seek out and respond effectively to necessary sources of its nourishment. All life forms are given their lives by means of proteins, which give structure and function to the cells of living organisms, but they can do so only through the interactions of RNA and DNA molecules, and the detailed instructions these interactions impart to the cells.

The instructions of these two molecules also account for regular asexual or sexual reproductions of the multifarious kinds of life on earth. Chance alterations of the instructions themselves or of changes in the numbers of new forms of such reproductions produced in this accidental way can also account for the emergence of new species of life.

How did life arise in the first place on earth? There are various theories purporting to account for this fact at present, but none of them has commanded universal consent. They key to the origin of life is the origin of the RNA and DNA molecules, and fundamental to life is the origin of the prokaryotic cells, the cells without a nucleus—as in the case of bacteria—as well as of those that have nuclei, namely, the eukaryotic cells that figure prominently in other kinds of life. All of these observations are familiar to us today, but they give emphasis to my conviction that emergent time, working with matter-energy, has produced everything around us here on earth and in our present universe as a whole—from the simplest to the most complex *atoms* and the *molecules* made up of these atoms—to the simplest and most complex types of *life*, including the type of our own human species. Each of these life forms has a teleological character, as I have frequently noted. With this fact in mind, I want to turn in the next section to the evolutionary origin of nonhuman life forms capable of various kinds and degrees of *consciously intentional* telic modes of thought and behavior.

Nonhuman Types of Conscious Life

I have been describing *how* life evolved, not *why* it evolved. The *why* issue assumes that there is, or should be, some kind of overall account or satisfying explanation provided for a supposed all-inclusive purpose of the evolution of life on earth. If we propose as an answer to the latter question, "Because life is a means to adaptation and survival," this is only an extension of the *how* question, because it only poses the issue of how nature works in the ways it does in such a manner as to produce creatures with a distinctively new means of survival. There would be no point in creating such creatures in the first place if they were not made fit to survive. Nature is a system that by its nature creates a prolific number of things and particular kinds of things. The living ones we are capable of knowing anything about are the ones that have survived, at least through limited periods of time.

How nature does so we can at least partially explain. Why it does so, we have no idea, because we would be asking "Why is there such a thing as nature itself, with all of its contents, coming and going, and with all of its regular, immanent, lawlike principles as well as its accidental features?" But responding to the *how* question is the best we can do and all that we need to do unless we want to resort to something other than nature in order to provide an answer to the *why* one. Then we simply move the question back one level, forcing us to ask why the existence of this other allegedly more fundamental end-seeking and acting principle, force, being, or beings can be explained. Either that, or we attribute consciously intended purposes to nature itself, making it not only the source of life but consciously alive in its own right, which seems to be quite a stretch.

American philosopher Lawrence Cahoone makes the crucial point I am seeking to express with these words: "It should be noted that emergence does not explain; it is the name of an apparent fact, a description. If one asks why is there emergence, I have no answer other than to say that the values of the physical constants of the universe, along with physical laws, have apparently made evolution with novel properties—physical, chemical, and biological evolution—likely" (Cahoone 2019: 162). This is an approach to the topic of teleology that I want us to keep constantly in mind. The fact that nature has caused teleological beings to emerge does not require that we attribute a teleological end, goal, or purpose to nature itself.

Let us keep this fact in mind as we move to discussion of nonhuman life forms that have emerged with at least some degree of conscious intentionality and purpose, and then onto ourselves as conscious human selves. We are undeniably conscious and capable of being keenly, alertly, complexly so. But nature as such is not. We can ask and answer all sorts of questions about consciously intended actions and expect, at least in most cases, to find reasonable answers to those questions. But they have no reasonable place or function when we ask them of nature itself unless we think of nature as guided or pervaded by some kind of overarching intention or purpose.

If we do the latter, as theists or some kinds of nontheistic panpsychists are wont to do, then we have to raise the why questions again in relation to the divine conscious being (or beings, as in the case of polytheism) or set of panpsychist presuppositions. But at least we would then presumably be dealing with something having conscious intentions or an assumed framework of ideal ends. I do neither of these and stick, therefore, with the *how* questions when it comes to nature and our place as emergent intentional beings within nature.

The *how* questions admittedly raise questions of meaning and value. I find meanings and values amply present in nature and in my life as a natural being. But I do not regard them as put there by some nonnatural, meta-natural, or supernatural source. There is no purpose *of* nature, as I continue to affirm, but there are ample meanings, values, and purposes available to us *in* nature, as I shall argue in the section after this one. But first let me say a bit more about the principle focus of this section, which is the evolutionary emergence of the many kinds and degrees of conscious nonhuman life forms in nature.

All kinds and degrees of consciousness among life forms, whenever and wherever it emerges in nature, have adaptive values. They are means whereby living beings of various kinds can adapt successfully to their natural environments and be capable of thriving and surviving in those environments. This observation accounts for the fact of their being so many life forms that are conscious in varying degrees, although none of them appears to have the exceptionally alert, resourceful, and constructive kind of consciousness possessed by humans. Consciousness is present in all such cases, with its adaptive function, and it is manifested and has been made possible in many different ways among large numbers of the living creatures of nature.

As Todd E. Feinberg and Jon M. Mallatt in their book *Consciousness Demystified* point out, prior to the emergence of consciousness, responsiveness to the environment was limited to reflexive actions in many creatures, at first simple and then more complex, each such action or reaction made possible by relatively simple nervous systems. Then core brains evolved, enabling some additional basic survival functions. These central nervous systems with their core brains eventually made consciousness possible, with its adaptive advantages. This developmental process came to characterize many different kinds of life.

What, then, are the adaptive advantages of consciousness? The two authors stress such factors as its allowing for flexible behavior, flexible learning, dealing with new situations, predicting the near future and providing for error correction, and unified simulation or modeling of the environment that directs behavior in three-dimensional space and makes appropriate decisions possible (101–02). These decisions are responsive to the adaptive opportunities and demands of particular environments, and these opportunities and demands function as natural *values* that evoke and guide conscious choices.

Nature is profuse and extravagant in its generations of innumerably different kinds of life, and these kinds come increasingly to approach and then to achieve levels of conscious feeling, awareness, and response as ways of coping more efficiently and effectively with the challenges and dangers of being able to survive and thrive in different kinds of environment. Being *pro-life* and favoring many different kinds of life, nature is also *pro-conscious-ness*. Why is nature this way? There is no ready answer to this question, and there need not be. But we can provide plausible answers to another question: How or by what stages of change and development does nature become so?

Once nature has proliferated beings with increasingly complex and more highly developed degrees of consciousness, it shows itself capable, as a new stage of development, of producing us human beings with our own kind of consciousness. The real possibilities posed by the emergence of incre-mental stages of conscious life in the past made way for the emergence of the new actuality of conscious humans. These earlier creatures of emergent processes, with their different types of consciousness, include, according to Feinberg and Mallatt, all cephalopods (such as octopuses, squid, cuttlefish, and nautilus) and vertebrate creatures of countless different kinds. The two authors also include, more controversially, arthropods as examples of conscious invertebrate beings, and particularly bees (58–63). These inclusions imply that humans are far from being the only genuinely conscious life forms on the face of the earth. The "natural kind" of consciousness admits of many different types and degrees. They prepare the way for the emergence of human consciousness, the version of it we shall now discuss.

Conscious Human Life

Human consciousness is an astounding miracle of biological evolution. It is made possible by the emergence of human beings' central nervous system and extremely complex brain. In a 2021 *Scientific American* article, neuro-scientist Christof Koch discusses how experiments with electrical stimulation of regions of the brain can show where various kinds of responses and experiences can be awakened in different parts of the brain. Considerable progress in this regard has been achieved, and the article shows this to be the case in impressive detail. But *where* in the brain different kinds of experience can be located is different from the issue of *how* they are made possible. After indicating what can currently be known about the former issue, Koch readily admits how little we understand at present about the latter one: "The true Annapurna ahead involves understanding how three pounds of [electronically] excitable brain matter is responsible for seeing, moving, and suffering. Yes, the physical substrate of heaven and hell is rooted in bioelectrical signals that obey natural laws. But that tells us precious little about how a trillion electrical signals spiking each second, streaming over networks of tens of billions of heterogenous cells, constitute a sight, sound, or emotion." He concludes this meditation by asking, "What is it about the brain, the most complex piece of active matter in the known universe, that turns the activity of 86 billion neurons into the feeling of life itself?" (75).

We have seen that consciousness is not restricted to humans, but it has reached through evolutionary emergence over millions of years an exceptionally high stage of development in humans. And how it is made possible by the three-pound human brain in its relations to other parts of the human body remains, for the most part, an enticing and inexplicable mystery. This brain is the basis of the most impressive kind of teleology known to us here on earth, a teleology evolved from and crucially dependent on the matter-energy of the brain as a purely bodily production. From it arise all of the searching "why" questions of which humans have shown themselves to be capable over the centuries and millennia of their various cultures and civilizations. In it somehow resides the competencies of human conscious awareness, goal-directed behavior, and intentional freedom.

In the human brain also resides, I should not fail to note, the source of radically conflictual, and not just amicable, relations among human beings that have blighted and devastated their history through the ages. "All we like sheep have gone astray. We have turned every one to his own Way," moans the prophet Isaiah about his Israelite people, and the Psalmist despairingly wonders, "Why do the nations so furiously rage together, and why do the people imagine a vain thing?" These laments in Handel's oratorio *Messiah*, based on the biblical texts of Isaiah 53: 6 and Psalm 2: 1, give doleful testimony to this fact. Contentious, competitive, and sometimes violent self-centeredness, indifferent or hostile attitudes toward the wellbeing and just treatment of others, and hateful, destructive wars among tribes and nation-states have long been the blatant wounds of human history.

As a result humans have long sought ways of adapting peaceably, constructively, compassionately, and justly to one another—a further example of how evolution prompts adaptive behavior, in this case the continuing thoughtful search for ways to achieve and sustain such behavior. The search has resulted in progressive articulations of moral principles and attempts to build consensus about and achieve implementations of such principles among humans. This process has not only been encouraged in the attitudes, thoughts, and intentions of individuals but has also been incorporated into social and political institutions of human cultures. It has been possible because of the evolution of beings capable of high levels of intentional reflection, analysis, choice, and action.

The values arrived at in these ways are clearly adaptive in their nature and can be regarded as discoveries of values made possible by nature itself, as nature is represented in the lives of nature's human creatures in their relations to one another and to their natural environments. Religions at their best have also helped immeasurably in aiding this process of moral sensitization, as have the various kinds of artistic expression that appeal to deep levels of human imagination and feeling, not just to the strictly rational, analytic abilities of humans. The social sciences have made their important contributions of analysis and understanding as well. There is teleology aplenty in the ongoing lives of human beings, and this teleology is very much a part of nature. We need to look nowhere else to account for it and to recognize it as an emergent rather than primordial fact about our lives in the world.

But does not the search for such values, the ongoing discoveries of them, and at least some success in their implementation by human cultures and civilizations, imply that nature itself is currently and has always been a teleological system, thus giving credence and support to Nagel's position? In order correctly to answer this question, we need to make a basic distinction between two quite different ways of thinking. The first is Nagel's way of wanting to brand teleology as primordial, and the second is regarding teleology as not primordial but emergent—as coming into being over immense expanses of time. Nature does so by evolving teleological beings on earth, not by incorporating from the outset a teleological character.

But what about the adaptive *values* required for the appropriate functioning of these teleological beings? Are these not already resident in nature? In response to this question, we need to see that these values are not primordial but come into being only as life forms find ways to adapt successfully to the pressures and exigencies of their natural environments. The values do not so much already reside in nature as come into being within the *relations* of organisms to their environments. The locus of these values, in other words, is neither solely in nature itself nor in the creatures of nature but in the ways these creatures come to adjust and accommodate themselves to their environments and to one another in order to survive and thrive, the members of each species doing so in their own distinctive ways. Viewed in this way, there are no values as such in nature prior to the evolution of its multitudinous life forms. The values come into being as these life forms evolve and later in the evolutionary saga become able *consciously* to search for and find ways of adapting successfully to their environmental settings and to other life forms within those settings.

Furthermore, this process does not arrive at a once-and-for-all accomplishment but requires unending struggles for resolutions in constantly changing environmental circumstances and, particularly, in the continuously changing circumstances of human cultures over millennia. Where are the values required for guiding the teleological lives of living beings? They exist neither in nonliving nor living nature alone but only as the latter come into being over time and, in the process of doing so, adjust to the opportunities and demands of their environments. In doing so, these life forms *bring values into being* as necessary aspects of their teleological functioning.

Values emerge, therefore, even as life does, and they increasingly gain susceptibility of recognition and response on earth with the emergence of beings capable of increasing degrees of consciousness—a process that has reached its highest phase of development at present with the evolution of Homo sapiens. Is nature a teleological system here on earth? The proper answer, as I regard it, is this: yes, it now is, in the sense just described. It was not originally so but became so with the evolution of life on earth. And it became more obviously and indisputably so with the evolution of conscious life, where increasingly intentional quests for and recognitions of values fit to inform and guide these lives became possible. The teleological thought, behavior, searches for, and commitment to values for guiding the course of life have become unmistakable in the lives of human beings. And the teleology I speak of throughout in this book is not some kind of determinism or compatibilism but a developing teleology of genuinely free thought and action.

Conclusion

Nature has no discernible, overall, primordial purpose for its being. It just is what it is, the product of the conjectured Big Bang and, behind that, of the two primordials of matter-energy and time. But nature is the source of the prolific life forms on earth and of the ways in which they adapt to and flourish within their natural environments. It has brought them into being by means of its unceasing emergentist or evolutionary processes. These processes have operated in lawlike ways that exhibit the first meaning of telos discussed in this chapter: attainment of regular, repetitive, expected stages and outcomes. But these processes have also produced novel outcomes, millions of which have become startlingly new over the passage of great stretches of time. Such novel outcomes have included the emergence of innumerable forms of life.

A portion of the living creatures of this passage have become extinct over time, while newer ones have continued to evolve. Among the latter are those that have even acquired various degrees of consciousness, self-direction, and intentionality as ways of responding to the prospects and demands of their natural environments. Hence, nature can rightly be called a "blind watchmaker," as biologist Richard Dawkins proclaimed with the arresting title of one of his books (Dawkins 1987), but its unforeseen, unintentional, undirected processes have brought a plethora of teleological beings into existence.

These conscious kinds of life, whether only vaguely affectively (or feelingly) so in the earliest cases or with additional traits of more clearly focused conscious ingenuity, problem-solving, and intelligence later on in others, have become capable of highly effective kinds of adaptation, survival, and flourishing in the process. With them have evolved, therefore, various degrees of intentional goal directedness and deliberate, self-guided purposiveness: the second meaning of telos brought to the fore in the chapter's discussions. But whether conscious or not, all forms of life have the trait of adapting to their environments and even altering their environments in ways favorable to themselves, and this fundamental trait has evolved into conscious and deliberate ways of doing so. This evolutionary creation of novel forms of life, including the increasing evolution of conscious forms, has reached a present peak of complexity, resourcefulness, and ingenuity with the evolution of the human species.

There is no purpose operative in the whole of nature as such in the phases, modes, and outcomes of biological evolution on earth. There is no meaningful answer to the question of why nature has continued to do so. In other words, teleology is not primordial in the way I have argued matter-energy and time to be. Instead, teleology is derivative. It has come into existence over time with the evolution of life itself and more explicitly and noticeably with the evolution of creatures with varying degrees of consciousness.

Thus the *why* question is not applicable to nature itself. In my view, it makes no sense to ask why nature as a whole exists and functions as it does. Nature's givenness has brought into life beings such as ourselves capable of asking *why* questions in different ways and seeking plausible answers to them. In doing so, we seek sustaining purposes or *telē* for our existence in our relations to one another and to other aspects of our natural environments. Nature's teleology, if we should want to call it that, is solely its "blind," nonintentional power of *originating* purposive, teleological forms of life such as ourselves. It has no *antecedent*, all-encompassing purpose or reason for being. It is replete with potential values appropriate to these purposes but is not itself the product or outcome of any cosmic purpose.

The second part of this statement is therefore no reason for arriving at Sartre's and traditional theists' conclusions that, without God to confer purposes on our lives from without, each of us has no other recourse than being required arbitrarily to *invent for ourselves*, with no prior contexts of purpose or value and with absolute, unguided, nihilistic freedom, meaning and value for the living of our lives. I am well aware that theists of the traditional kind will agree with this point of view and disagree ardently and adamantly with my denial of antecedent teleology for nature, insisting that we must ground our fundamental purposes and values in the support, guidance, and direction of an acclaimed Divine Creator of the universe and everything in it. I respect defenders of this view, even though I do not share it. There is wonder, majesty, and mystery enough in our experiences of nature to allow for such serious differences of outlook and conviction. But it is essential that we continually submit our respective outlooks to the courts of reason and experience.

We humans are especially persistent and increasingly competent in raising and resolving *how* questions about nature, namely, questions about how this or that part of nature's processes works. These *how* questions have led us to include in our insistent queries *why* questions about human existence, and we rightly do so. Why should we do this rather than that? Why should we live in this manner rather than that one? What choices and purposes can give substance, meaning, and purpose to our lives? What values should guide the responsible living of these lives, bounded as they are by the contingencies of our births and the inevitabilities of our coming deaths? In what ways ought human beings relate to one another and to the rest of nature?

However, we *mistakenly extend* such questions to the point of asking why nature itself exists, has produced our present universe, has brought the earth into being, has evolved life in its manifold forms, and created our species in the process. There are more than enough potential purposes and values to be sought for and aspired toward in the living of our lives and in our relations to the splendors and wonders of nature as well as to its daunting perplexities, tragedies, and terrors. The earth's teleology is altogether emergent and immanent and not primordial or transcendent, in my considered judgment, and there is no desperate hope or need for it to be any different. This is the thesis I have defended in the current chapter. I shall continue to explore, defend, and apply its implications in the chapters to follow.

Chapter Three

Teleology and Values

"Conceptual experience" is the entertainment of possibilities for ideal realization in abstraction from any sheer physical realization. . . . Life lies below this grade of mentality. Life is the enjoyment of emotion, derived from the past and aimed at the future. It is the enjoyment of emotion which was then, which is now, and which will be then. This vector character is of the essence of such entertainment.

—Alfred North Whitehead (1958: 229)

The "vector character" of which philosopher Alfred North Whitehead speaks in this epigraph, and which he attributes to all kinds of life, is another way of referring to life's *teleological* character. It is the anticipatory and purposive movement of organisms from their pasts, into their presents, and onward into their futures—a movement that it is their nature as living beings to exemplify. They encounter the future from their standpoints in the present as derived from their standpoints in the past in order to continue their development, sustenance, and existence into the future. Unlike rocks or other kinds of nonliving entities, they combine a kind of unconscious or conscious recollection and acknowledgment of their existence with a kind of unconscious or conscious impetus or aspiration to continue living and making the most of their lives. In this important sense, all kinds of life, from the most primitive to the most sophisticated, are teleological agents.

All life forms possess lower or higher grades of "mentality," to use Whitehead's term, and they are all oriented toward what they have yet to become as living beings interacting with and endeavoring to flourish within their environments. This flourishing is what I think Whitehead has in mind in using the terms *enjoyment* and *emotion*. The millions of specific life forms on earth deeply endeavor and act, as it were, in accordance with an indwelt zest for life. This zest requires them to face toward the needs, demands, and possibilities of their respective futures.

Without this forward-looking orientation they could not continue to exist. The orientation can be unconscious or largely so, in which case we could speak, instead of "emotion," of an unconscious "urge" or "impulse" toward self-realization and self-continuation. Were there no such urge, life would not be possible. Life is therefore inseparable from teleology, from some sort of future-oriented effort or striving, whether consciously entertained or not. Organisms strive toward the future. Boulders, plains, mountains, streams, and clouds do not. The latter *persist* in being over periods of time but they do not *strive* to be and become.

What organisms strive toward in their autopoietic, sense-making, and purposive manner, as we noted philosopher Evan Thompson to argue in chapter 1,[1] can rightly be called *values*. These are natural values essential to as well as contributory toward increasing degrees of conscious awareness and enjoyment as we scan the scale of the evolutionary emergence and development of sophisticated nervous systems. What are striven for and more consciously envisioned and pursued as goals for attainment—when more complex organisms and neuronal systems have evolved—eventually and in this manner become full-fledged and distinctively recognized *values*, acknowledged as such and aspired toward accordingly.

Teleological Character of Values

When so recognized and regarded, such values are teleological phenomena, natural ends pursued and routinely attained on earth. With the evolution of high levels of consciousness, especially notable in human beings with their large brain size relative to the size of their bodies, values become prominent features of everyday life—whether positive or negative in their notable attainments or in their regrettable violations and neglects. To make this observation, which is consistent with Whitehead's as well as with my own view, is simply to acknowledge how crucial values, seen as sought-for ends of quality and attainment, are to life forms on earth.

No commission of a so-called naturalistic fallacy is involved to arrive at this observation. We are not reasoning from detected facts to conjectured values, from mere "is" to speculative "ought."[2] Instead, we are taking account of the necessity of values in the course and pursuit of life itself. Life is teleological and purposeful in its very nature, and this makes it value oriented and value striving, whether consciously so or not. The bee values its queen, hive, nectar, and blossoms. The lion values its hunt and its cubs; the beaver its aspen trees, dams, and den; the bacterium its sugar; the tree its sun, soil, and rain—all enough to devote their lives—consciously or unconsciously—to these necessarily valued goals and ideals. Values in nature are neither problematic, rare, or absent. Instead, they are omnipresent in all forms of life. There would be no facts about life without a pervasive immanence of the pursuit of values in all living creatures.

Truth and value are not synonymous and should not be confused with one another. But the pursuit of truth has undeniable value and can lead to the refinement of old values or to the discovery of important new ones. Facts and values, and the discovery and articulation of either, while in some sense separate, are in another sense closely and undeniably conjoined—each suffusing and underlying the other. As Whitehead reflects, the conceptual investigations of humans have a vital role to play in the discovery and entertainment of visceral, valuative experiences. But without the profoundly felt desire to know truths about an immense multitude of things, there would be few truths recognized and known as such by humans. Animals must desperately yearn to know some truths in order to stay alive. These truths, once known, can have immense value for them. Values are neither purely conceptual nor purely visceral, but neither are truths, properly understood.

Another important thing to recognize about values is that they are relational. They do not just exist out in the world awaiting discovery. They come into being in relation to beings capable of experiencing value, and they exist only in that relationship. To borrow again Whitehead's analogy of the vector, they are recognized as such "there" from the perspective of "here" and most particularly "here and now." In other words, values, when properly conceived, are not abstract but concrete. And in many cases, they can be matters of life or death. In all cases, they are indispensable contributors to the quality of life, especially in the cases of beings with some modicum of conscious awareness.

Ultimate Source of Values

Where do values come from? Why are they so prolific on the face of the earth? My contention is that values are telic phenomena, and that such phenomena would not exist in the absence of life. Apart from life forms of some kind or other, multiple aspects of nature would pose potentialities for value, but there would be no actual values. In other words, potentialities for valuation become actual only when there are creatures capable of experiencing, responding to, and relating to them as values. Thus nature alive in the biospheres of earth is replete with values because it is replete with beings capable of and dependent on experiences of value—in a word, teleological creatures, creatures oriented toward and responsive to the necessity and lure of valuative ends.

But why is there such a thing as this earth of pervasive life with its valuative ends in view, or at least necessarily taken into account and responded to, by all living beings of whatever levels of response? If we answer, "Because it is in the nature of life to be valuational; this trait is essential to its continuation, flourishing, and survival," then I think we will have given a perfectly reasonable and adequate answer to the question. But if we persist in our questioning and raise a further one, "Why is there such a thing as life, with its inherent and indispensable trait of valuing its survival and those aspects of its environment necessary to its survival, as well as to its flourishing within the opportunities and constraints of its environment," then we raise not so much a *why* question as a *how* one, as I argued in chapter 2.

At some point, the *how* questions can only be resolved with something presumed to be sheerly given and with no need for further explanation. That point, in my view, is nature itself, not only in its character of nature *natured*—the present face of nature elsewhere as well as here on earth—but also its character as nature *naturing*, the billions of years of its processive creativity that we find to be so vividly illustrated in our current awareness of its cosmic, terrestrial, and biological evolutions.

My analysis and reasoning terminate here, because all such reasoning has to have a stopping point, the stage at which we can say that it is simply in the nature of things for there to be such. If we think that something more ultimate than nature is required, then we will say that this something is that more ultimate being, factor, or principle that itself requires no further explanation. But for me, it is *in the nature of nature* to be such or to have evolved as such. Nature is the given from which all else flows. It is metaphysically ultimate. I defend this claim in part 2 of my 2002 book *A Religion of Nature*. Thus it is the creative power of nature, at least on earth and probably elsewhere in the present universe, that originates life and, with life, teleology itself and teleological goals, ends, and values of many different kinds.

All forms of life are teleological in some respects and degrees. We know, or feel confident that we know today, how or by what incremental processes life has reached its prolific character on earth—even though we are not completely sure how it originated in the first place. We have different theories about how to answer this last question but have reached no satisfying consensus. It does make sense to me to conclude that however life first arose on earth, its origination and evolution fully explain the teleological phenomena of earth that turn on the necessarily valuative, end-oriented character of life itself.

I know that this stopping point of analysis and reasoning is far from satisfactory to some, but if not, it will require another kind of stopping point that will seem as arbitrary or unsatisfying to others. The debate between antecedent and consequent, primordial or derivative teleology goes on. I opt for the "derivative" side of this debate.

Teleology is the *outcome* of natural processes that have given rise to life on earth. It is not their primordial basis or original generative source. Furthermore, life itself is not primordial. It is the outcome of matter-energy interacting with time. In order to understand this statement, we need to remind ourselves that time is not mere uninterrupted continuity but a blend of continuity and novelty. Each new moment of time, at least to some degree, is unique—a new moment or phase of the flow of time. This fact is what warrants our calling it "new." Were it not, there would be no such thing as the flow of time. The novelty implicit in the flow of time can, over stretches of time, bring new physical or matter-energy things into being. And if the stretch is long enough, life can and has come into being—first in very simple forms and then in increasingly more complex forms as time goes on. Thus does teleology on earth and probably elsewhere in the universe become real. And with teleology, values of different sorts as its implicit teleological ends or goals also make their entry.

What are some of the basic types of value that we find in nature as human beings? There are at least four major ones of these, and I discuss each of them in turn in the following sections. The four are self-value; other-value; the values of earth, sea, and sky; and the sacred majesty of the universe.[3]

Self-Value

Every organism on earth has implicit self-value in the sense that it seeks, whether consciously or not, for its own maintenance and preservation over the course of its life. Without this value, it would not persist in living. The same is true of at least the ordinary, everyday lives of human beings. An overwhelmingly strong counter motivation is needed to act in defiance of this value and to have recourse to suicide, which helps to explain why suicide is such an extreme, abnormal act. In most circumstances, it is an act of despair that flies in the face of the normally assumed, hopeful value of self-affirmation. In less usual cases, it is the willing sacrifice of the value of one's own life in order to insure something that a person considers to be of greater value than the person's self-preservation in particular circumstances, such as saving the life of someone else in imminent danger, radically endangering one's life in order to prevent a glaring atrocity, regularly putting one's life at grave risk in warfare because of a powerful sense of duty and love of country, and so on.

What philosophical theologian Paul Tillich calls "the courage to be" in his perceptive book with this title (1952), is the manifestation of what I am calling self-value. It is quite ordinary rather than rare despite the courage it requires—usually in the face of all odds—because valuing one's own life and doing whatever one can to preserve it and maximize its possibilities are essential to the ongoingness and meaningfulness of life. Each of us is a gift of oneself to oneself, a gift that offers only a finite span of time in which to accomplish what one can in the way of other important values throughout one's life. At the age of ninety, as I write this sentence, I am keenly aware of the compelling urgency of this finite span.

We humans are in general hopefully intent on trying to make the most of the challenges and opportunities our individual lives set before us. When this intention lapses, is neglected, or is radically interfered with, we usually feel a kind of haunting remorse, regret, and unease—the distressing sense of an indispensable value woefully ignored, misused, or violated. The will to live and to live well, on the one hand, and the valuation of the gift of oneself to oneself, on the other, are not separable from one another. Whatever routinely interferes with or prevents the continuing aspirations and activities of appropriate self-love on the part of an individual human being or of any group of human beings is commonly—and certainly ought to be—seen as a tragic erosion of bedrock natural value.

This interference is self-inflicted in some cases and may not admit of clear explanation. But in many cases it is at least to a large extent the effect of such factors as neglectful or malicious parenting, condescending and hateful racial or other kinds of prejudice and ill-use on the part of others, severe poverty, chronic homelessness, crushing loneliness, lack of cultural opportunities such as a good education or the availability of a fulfilling job, a crushing sense of personal failure, a seriously debilitating physical or mental illness, or an incapacitating addiction to alcohol or drugs. Severe self-rejection is the rare exception that proves the rule of generally taken for granted self-value. Such self-value is characteristic of all living creatures. In humans, it is an unmistakable basic value, even if not always a fully or even partially realized one.

Other-Value

We humans as natural beings are by our very nature social beings. Other-value, and not merely self-value, is built into us by nature, not something imposed on us from above or requiring explanation by something other than our inherent character as creatures of nature. But it is not in isolation that we become aware of our social nature. It is in community. We humans, in the words of philosopher John Dewey, "traverse a spiral in which social customs generate some consciousness of interdependencies, and this consciousness is embedded in acts which in improving the environment generate new perceptions of social ties, and so on forever. The relationships, the interactions are forever there as fact, but they acquire meaning only in the desires, judgments and purposes they awaken" (1981: 721). In other words, moral values are ineluctably social and not primarily individual. They are awakened in community, critiqued and tested in community, brought to the attention of individuals in community, and so on continuously.

This process begins in childhood, typically with parents (or a parent) and family into which a child is born, and continues throughout human life. Individuals can respond to and reflect on the moral values of social groups and contribute to their improvement. But they do not create them at first hand. The human communities from which they take their origins and within which they operate are functions of nature because human beings are creatures of nature, not beings outside of or set over against nature. No external teleological source or sanction is either involved or required. Other-value is a fact of nature, and it is born and sustained in community—in our necessary relations to one another as human beings.

But as we are becoming increasingly aware today, other-value does not stop with the human community. It extends outward to include community with all life forms on earth. We crucially depend on them, and they crucially depend on us. We, like them, are ecological beings, beings intimately related not only to our fellow humans but to the whole biosphere of nature on earth. Nature is a system of necessary interdependencies, and we are integral parts of that system. Our moral obligations to nonhuman creatures have their basis in the natural fact of our necessary relations with one another. There is no need for further or deeper explanation of their binding power. We are committed to the presence of other-values because we must be. It is true that we can endeavor to overlook or be oblivious to this fact, but we do so only at the cost of our own endangerment as a species of life, to say nothing of such an endeavor's endangerments to innumerable other species on earth today.

Such obliviousness is as ridiculous and indefensible as would be the liver saying to the stomach, or the brain to the heart, "I have no need of you and no obligation to contribute anything to your wellbeing." A chain is only as strong as its weakest link, and we humans must guard against becoming the perilously weak link of fatal pride and indifference when it comes to the whole of nature on earth in its present ecological crisis. Thoughtful, intensive, urgent care for the wellbeing of earth and its creatures in our time is not some haughty act of condescending noblesse oblige on the part of human beings but action of urgent necessity—for our own sake as well as for the sake of the other creatures in the earth's intricately interwoven web of life.

My wife Pam and I were wandering along a small lake with our binoculars. We spotted off in the distance along the shore of the lake a roseate spoonbill, with its bill flattened at the tip in the shape of a spoon and its plumage a spectacular pink. We had never witnessed this particular creature at the lake near our home in the Big Bend area of northern Florida, and its sight filled us both with intense appreciation for the privilege of witnessing this splendid fellow creature, quietly walking, hunting, and feeding along the lake's weedy shore. Our reaction to its unexpected presence was a sense of gratitude for its being a part of our world on earth, and a recognition of its inestimable value as part of the vast community of earthly creatures with which we humans are tightly bound, interdependent members. It is a wonderous community, but it is also an ambiguous one, marked by many natural perils, including the perils of predation, starvation, disease, destruction of habitat, and the like. And we humans can augment and increasingly have augmented these perils through our technology and through indifference to its effects on the natural environments of our fellow creatures on earth.

We share with all of these creatures the earth's largess and grandeur, and there is no moral justification for any of us humans to extract and exploit its riches at the radical expense of one another or of them, or to fundamentally threaten one another's or their ongoing flourishings and lives. To do so, attempt to do so, or allow to become so are flagrant *disvalues*, violations of the interlocking values of our lives on earth. It is an injustice of which we humans are patently guilty at present, a sad misuse of our estimable gifts of intelligence and freedom. We threaten not only the lives of such creatures as the splendid roseate spoonbill but the lives of all the humble, less spectacular—at least to our impressionistic, immediate view—creatures on which their lives as well as our own depend. We should also not forget that every drop of water in which the spoonbill wades teems with microscopic, normally unnoticed forms of life. I shall never forget my first astonishing encounter with this fact through a microscope in my late adolescence.

There are perils and losses enough in nature without our adding to them with our current ecological sins of commission and omission. We are not custodians of the earth, entitled to make use of it any way that we wish or see fit. We are only humble members of an enormous community of living creatures, much more dependent for our lives on insects, for example, than they are on us. This community is a thing of immense value to us and to them. It is a telic value in its own right and does not require conferral of value from elsewhere to qualify as such. Nor does it have to have some kind of immanent, nonderivative, panpsychical character to be recognized as such. Its values are relational ones, the relations of living beings to the day-to-day resources the earth thankfully provides them for the living and flourishing of their lives, human and nonhuman alike. These precious resources are delicate and all too easily squandered and left out of mind by humans. That is the pressing peril of our time.

Earth, Sea, and Sky

It is not just our individual selves, our lives with other humans, and our interdependent relations to nonhuman forms of life that command our deepest respect and response as natural values needing no more ultimate teleological explanation than that which they themselves provide. The non-living parts of earth, sea, and sky as observed from our terrestrial perspective also have this role in and of themselves when our feelings and minds are properly attuned to their incalculable value. The earth has given rise to life and sustains it wherever it exists, which is on the highest and lowest latitudes of its surface, at the shallowest and lowest depths of its seas, and across the widest expanses of its winged air.

Poets of immemorial time have been well aware of the values of the earth itself, values implicit in the nature of life on this planet, as its individual life forms have striven toward self-preservation and self-fulfillment, and as life has exhibited its evolutionary development through much of the planet's history. The earth's soils, seas, and skies have nurtured and sustained these innumerable life forms, providing for the predominant aerobic ones the oxygen they breathe, whether in the water or in the air; the food on which all of them depend, whether by herbivory or predation; the water they must continuously imbibe or absorb in order to remain alive; and the very materials out of which their bodies are formed. To say that life crucially relies on the resources provided by the earth, and that earth has immense value for all kinds of life for this very reason, is a truism, even though an extremely important one.

But earth also has immense value in its own right, quite apart from its origin and support of life. Its necessary relations to life have brought recognition of these values to the fore, but they have always been there potentially, awaiting such recognition. I have in mind the splendor of white-crested ocean waves crashing onto a shore; the beauty of sunlit cumulus clouds floating in a cerulean sky; the fields of grain swaying nonchalantly in a summer's breeze; the towering sublimity of snow-capped mountains; the vista of grassy plains spreading to the horizon in the glow of a settling sun; the haunting lure of a shadowy forest; the bubbling stream frolicking across strewn rocks through its channel of verdant banks; the numinous flashes of lightning and awesome crashes of thunder; the vision of far-off moon, planets, and stars tirelessly wending their way across the velvet dome of the nighttime sky.

All such ordinary and yet, on due reflection, extremely *extraordinary* phenomena are things of great and even overwhelming importance and value when encountered and contemplated with a receptive spirit. Their values may have become obscured simply because they are so regularly and commonly experienced as soon to be in danger of being taken for granted. But such values are undeniably there, as poets and other sensitive artists remind us; as religiously attuned meditators, mythmakers, and symbol creators bring forcefully to our attention; and as all of those who make the effort and take the time to properly observe and ponder them soon discover. Packed with potential values of countless different sorts, the earth opens itself to appropriate responses of evaluation and action. Those who pause to think about their lives on earth and properly to appreciate them are prompted to exclaim—at least in my humble view, "This earth is my home, my country, my native land. All that I need in the way of values is here, not in some other vaguely dreamed-of, wistfully longed-for, unearthly realm!"

To discover, take into account, affirm, and put into practice these values is no easy task. It is especially difficult for those who have not had full opportunity to appreciate these earthly values and incorporate them into their lives for various reasons, including debilitating sickness, early death, loss of loved ones, accidents, calamitous natural disasters, rampant social and political injustices, and the like. These are tragedies of nature or evils of human malpractice made possible by nature. They should not be forgotten by those who happen to be more fortunate. Life on earth is full of potential values, but it is also susceptible to tragedy and grief. We humans, like all earthly creatures, are finite and live in a finite, ambiguous world. Our freedom to do good also includes our freedom to do evil, and in far too many cases, *monstrous* evil. Value and the potentiality of disvalue go hand in hand in a finite world—a poignant but necessary fact for us to keep constantly in mind as citizens of the earth.

Sacred Majesty of the Universe

Far beyond our earth and its relatively tiny solar system stretches the immensity of the Milky Way galaxy of which it is only a miniscule part, and far beyond this galaxy are millions of other ones extending to the most distant reaches of outer space. The universe made known to us by current science is so enormous, so astounding in the stories scientists tell us of its origins and developments, as to challenge our most fertile and focused imaginations.

Is it also a thing of value? It assuredly is, and not only from an aesthetic standpoint, as compellingly important as that is. Like the ecosystems of earth, every aspect of this incredibly vast universe is connected in some essential ways with innumerable other aspects. Its gravitational forces hold everything together even as the expansionary force of its dark energy continues to drive the whole system of its galaxies, stars, planets orbiting elliptically around the stars—its planetoids, asteroids, cosmic dust, and the like—further out into space, like some incredibly vast, continuously inflating balloon.

We can talk about the universe, theorize concerning the available evidence of its character, inner workings, and immensity. And we can attempt to describe and even to explain the processes that have produced and sustain it, but we cannot even begin concretely to picture many of these things. They lie beyond the scope of our puny imaginations. The universe's immensity has, in and of itself, a *sublimity* that weighs on the heart so profoundly as to be inexpressibly wondrous and must be recognized and experienced as something of intense and incalculable value. The universe in which we humans are privileged to live is marvelous in all of its aspects, whether spectacularly large or infinitesimally small—from the farthest rotating galaxies with their complements of billions of stars to the tiniest pulses of subatomic energy, and all the wonder, amazement, and delight that lie between these extremes of the unimaginably great and indescribably small. We live in a universe not only of astonishing facts but also of contagious and often spectacular values.

But our universe is not static. It continues to change and develop and has done so since its currently reasoned Big Bang origin. Some of the most fundamental of its laws or basic regularities and functionings had to be present at this origin and were there because of their role in the residue of a previous universe whose collapse created the ingredients of the Big Bang. These fundamental traits were then carried over into our emerging new universe. But they gave rise, in turn, to new laws pertaining to the forces, constituents, relations, and systems brought into being by this ongoing emergence. Why do I reason in this manner? I do so because I hold time to be primordial, meaning, among other things, that there is never an absolute beginning of anything, including our present universe. In other words, despite the insistent claim of some contemporary physicists, time does not begin with the Big Bang nor will it ever end, no matter what becomes of the present universe.[4] All of the possibilities of change and development in the universe, moreover, are *real*, not *pure*, possibilities. By this statement, I mean possibilities posed by past actualities, which have come into being on the basis of other past actualities, and so on back into endless time. The primordial character of time, along with the primordial character of matter-energy, are for me the most remarkable values of all, the ones that have made and continue to make all of the rest of them available to our recognition and response.

The values inherent in nature as we experience and reflect upon them—and as I have briefly indicated some of them here—give notice of what for me is a sacred world, a world richly deserving of profound religious reverence, faith, and commitment. Nature is the source of all life on earth. It creates us and sustains us. It contains millions of life forms and the systems of their interactions and interdependencies with which we humans are an integral part. It surrounds us with unlimited mystery and wonder, and can fill us with feelings of unspeakable awe. Its immensity beyond our earth and relatively tiny solar system astounds us and defies our imagination.

Proper attention to our multiple dependencies on nature can bless our lives, but failure to be responsible participants in its processes and respecters of its multitude of other kinds of life pose grave dangers to our individual lives as humans as well as to the continuation of our cultures and the survival of our civilization on the face of the earth. My most recent detailed descriptions, celebrations, and warnings concerning the sacredness of nature are contained in chapters 6 and 8 of my book *Sacred and Secular: Response to Life in a Finite World* (2022a). With humble respect and thankfulness for the great Jewish and Christian faiths but also with my own boldness of conviction, I paraphrase and adopt, as a proponent of Religion of Nature, two small parts of the Hebrew Bible: "The earth belongs to *nature*, and the fulness thereof / the world and those who dwell therein" (Psalm 24: 1) and "This is the day *nature* has made; / Let us rejoice and be glad in it" (Psalm 118: 24). The nature of which I speak is teleological by virtue of the innumerable teleological, living beings it contains here on earth, if not elsewhere or even throughout the present universe. With the teleological capabilities of these beings, which include us humans, go the abundant values with which we are surrounded and to which we are motivated to respond—each in its own manner—as appropriate ends, goals, or *telē*. The values that I have indicated and discussed in this chapter can function for each of us humans as fundamental sources, motivations, and focuses of a profoundly meaningful human life.

Conclusion

In this chapter, I have endeavored to explain the close connection between teleology and values, showing that teleology presupposes values as the targets of its forward-reaching, purposive tendencies, impulses, and aspirations. I have described four of the most salient classes of values available to us humans here on earth and stressed their great importance for the living of our lives. I have explained why I think that these purposes and values do not require a source beyond or outside of nature but reside wholly within, and can be entirely accounted for, by nature itself, with no need of recourse to anything supernatural and with no need to suppose some kind of primordial, nonderivative panpsychical character of nature.

I have proposed that two primordials are sufficient to explain all else in the universe in which we humans presently reside, namely, matter-energy and time. I have argued that the universes sequentially and everlastingly brought into being by these two primordials are all that there is or ever will be, but also that this is all there need be and that an attempt to begin to comprehend and take into account even parts of it is the work of many lifetimes. In other words, we live in a many-splendored, inexhaustibly value-laden, and awesomely sacred world and have no need to pine for another.

In arguing for the presence of innumerable kinds of values available to us humans in our lives here on earth, I have not opted for any kind of "is-ought" or so-called naturalistic fallacy. I do not reason from valueless facts to claims to value. Instead, I call attention to facts of value present throughout nature that need only *recognition* and not *inference* for convincing evidence of their presence throughout nature as we experience it. I do not claim that values are created by acts of evaluation, as though the mere valuing of something would be sufficient to make it a genuine value. Were this the case, valuing thievery, envy, resentment, hatefulness, lying, murder, cheating, destructive exploitation of natural resources, and the like would admittedly make them *ends* of behavior but could not give them the status of genuine *values*.

We can be mistaken about values just as we can be mistaken about facts. And we discover values in our relations to nature as natural beings just as we discover facts. Both kinds of discovery are essential aspects of our lives and of all other forms of life. Most importantly of all, I have argued for the inviolable but also the inexhaustible and inexpressible sacredness of nature—a sacredness that commands our utmost humble, reverent, grateful, and vigilant responses at all times and in all places. We need to be intensely aware of this sacredness in our perilous time of acute ecological disruption and danger here on earth.

Chapter Four

Evolutionary Origin and Development of Telic Values

Surely the mitochondrion that first entered another cell was not thinking about the future benefits of cooperation and integration; it was merely trying to make its own living in a tough Darwinian world. Accordingly, this fundamental step in the evolution of multicellular life arose for an immediate reason quite unrelated to its eventual effect upon organic complexity. This scenario seems to portray fortunate contingency rather than predictable cause and effect.

—Stephen Jay Gould (1989: 310)

The telic values, terrestrial and nonterrestrial, described in the previous chapter arose not merely as the outcome of rigorous causal laws and determinations, but also because of perennial accidents or contingencies—developments that did not have to occur as they did and might well have turned out differently. The value of life itself, as it has existed in the past and exists today in such prolific variety on the face of the earth, is the result of the interworkings of causality and contingency, of predictable laws and unpredictable chance occurrences. A central factor of *luck* must therefore be included in the explanation of our existence as humans on earth, and this factor is required to account for the existence here of all forms of earthly life.

Causality is an indisputable value, because without it, the universe would have no dependable order or possibility of being anything other than sheer chaos. But contingency is also a fundamental value, because without it there would be no such thing as development or change, including those

73

evolutionary changes that have produced our universe, our galaxy, its solar system, the planet earth, and the presence of life on earth. And without life, there would be no vectors of value crucial to the survival and flourishing of life forms on earth, as we have seen.

In the epigraph to this chapter, biologist Stephen Jay Gould takes note of one of the most remarkable of these contingent events on earth, namely, the entrance at a particular stage of evolutionary history of a certain kind of prokaryotic cells, or cells without a nucleus, into the nuclei of then existing eukaryotic cells, creating there the *mitochondria* of those cells. This contingent development had a tremendous effect on the evolution of later forms of life.

Mitochondria in biological organisms have such crucial functions as the conversion of food into usable energy, the transport and storage of calcium ions, the production of an iron compound in the blood that enables it to bring oxygen to the body's tissues, and the creation of basic hormones such as estrogen and testosterone. More complex life forms would not have developed as they routinely have without the contingent, nonnecessary migration—at a certain point in evolutionary history—of prokaryotic cells that developed into the essential mitochondria of what became their host eukaryotic cells. An interesting discussion of the critical role played by mitochondria in the cells of the human body for the transmission and utilization of energy, including the myriad electrical impulses required for consciousness and cognition, is provided in Nick Paumgarten's 2021 *New Yorker* essay.

This is but one of innumerable examples that could be cited of the continuing role of contingency or chance in the evolution of life as we know it today. And as we saw in previous chapters, there would be no recognition or appropriation of potentialities for value apart from life, and no such thing as teleology. Teleology, values, and life are necessarily connected with one another—and all three are emergent, not primordial, phenomena. Like every aspect of the present universe, they provide evidence of the dynamic character of the universe that marks it at every stage of its development. This dynamic character exhibits, in my view, the interactions of matter-energy and time—the two primordials of the metaphysical outlook I endorse and defend.

Nature is not only something presently naturated (*natura naturata*) but is also something continually evolving and changing (*natura naturans*). In making this observation, I do not mean to posit any kind of dualism. Nature naturated or the present face of nature on earth and elsewhere in the universe is the current product of nature naturing. Process and product go naturally together and can be neither conceptually nor actually separated from one another. There would be no dynamism in nature were there no such thing as chance or contingency as that is continually manifested by its role in the passage of time, when time is properly understood as a combination of continuity and novelty. In all of these ways, teleology, telic values, causality and contingency, relative stasis and ongoing change, are tied together—along with the two primordials of matter-energy and time.

This is the central thesis of this book, and from it follows a coalescence of different kinds of value that can be regarded as the foci of purposive activity on earth. I discussed four classes of such values in chapter 3. I now want to focus more specifically on three valuative issues that confront us humans with special urgency today: the fate of the earth and its nonhuman creatures, the fate of human beings on earth, and the prospect of human freedom and hope. Directions and rates of change in all three of these areas are not entirely predictable. In fact, each area is in grave danger as an aspect of the global ecological crisis of today.

We humans have a critical and even decisive role to play in all three of these areas because we are formidable agents of change for good or ill on the face of the earth. We are such because of our freedom, a force for change that supplements chance or contingency with significant effects on the direction of events on earth—whether by freedom's salutary uses or by its uncaringly destructive ones. Many other creatures of earth have freedom to some extent as well, but humans have it to an exceptional degree and are thus capable of affecting their own future, the futures of other creatures of earth, and the integrity of these creatures' habitats and ecosystems in fundamental and far-reaching ways. The concept of nature naturing and of the earth's susceptibility to ongoing favorable or unfavorable change includes, therefore, acts of individual and collective human freedom that can bring and currently are bringing about enormous changes on the face of nature as we witness and experience it here on earth.

Human beings are therefore momentous participants in and agents of nature naturing on earth in our time. As such, we are capable of bringing about massive changes in the fates of earth's living creatures—human and nonhuman alike—in their natural environments, as well as in the earth's overall character. Here is both a peril of telic values and an opportunity of telic values. Here the importance of a proper understanding of the character and power of human teleology in the philosophy of nature as it pertains to earth, and as life on earth, comes inescapably into view. Potentialities for the intentional incorporation and maintenance of positive values throughout the earth are also potentialities for radical disvalues.

Both kinds of potentiality and of their intentional actualizations by living beings are outcomes of biological evolution and its central aspects of chance and novelty, not of something always preexisting, underlying, or predetermining its character and outcomes. Such evolution creates teleological beings and their values throughout nature on earth, and in this fact lies both teleology's welcome benefits and its grave dangers.

Actualizations of the latter kinds of potentiality are becoming increasingly evident today, and I want now to indicate two basic ways in which this observation is unfortunately true. The "fate" with which I designate these two areas is not meant to mark them as inevitable, because both continue to be subject to the free acts of human beings. But I do mean to lay heavy stress on the undeniably serious and fateful character of each area on which so much depends. At some point each is in grave danger of becoming *irrevocably* harmful and destructive. Each gives evidence of the crucial importance of the teleological capabilities of humans that are effects of their evolution as a biological species. In the next two sections, I will discuss the fate of the earth and its nonhuman creatures and the fate of humans and of their freedoms and hopes.

Fate of the Earth and Its Nonhuman Creatures

There are far too many regrettable ways in which humans have besmirched and despoiled the earth, which is their home as one of its natural beings. Their industries, power plants, factory farms, refineries, transportation systems, mines, and the like have pumped pollutants into the ground, air, rivers, and seas—thus threatening many forms of life, including the lives of humans themselves. Pollutants in the atmosphere such as carbon dioxide and methane have produced a greenhouse effect, with resultant global warming, acidification of the seas, melting of glaciers and ice sheets, and release of more carbon dioxide and methane by thawing permafrost in high latitudes. Humans have also endangered many of earth's species of life by introducing invasive species into areas of the earth; by encroachments into the habitats of already present species; by poaching, hunting, or fishing existent species to extinction or near extinction; and, in general, by an all too common indifference toward forms of life and qualities of life on earth other than their own.

The teleological enhancement of a human power for great goodness is also a power for great evil. Neither side of this equation should ever be minimized or forgotten, and this advice holds especially true for the adjective "great" on both its sides. The statement bears closely on the topic of human freedoms and hopes to be discussed later in this chapter. What humans have the frightful power to undo, they also have the formidable power to respect, preserve, and maintain—a power that will not exist forever but endures at least for a limited time. The temptation to ignore, rationalize, or procrastinate must be firmly resisted. Paradoxically, not to choose is also a choice. It can turn out to be a fatal choice, not only for countless other forms of life but for the human one as well. *Urgency* is therefore the watchword.

It is all too easy for humans to assume that their fate is independent of the fates of other parts of nature on earth, that no matter what might happen elsewhere on this planet, humans can always find ways to triumph and endure. This is a delusion. It is such because all of the creatures of earth are tightly bound together, and because of the ruinous consequences the human part of nature already has had and therefore obviously can have for the whole of nature on earth. We learn this essential lesson from the science of ecology, which among many other things teaches us that we humans are integral parts of the earth's biosphere, a tightly wound skein of countless ecological systems and ecological dependencies.

Fate of the Human Creatures of Earth and of Their Freedoms and Hopes

Are things already too far gone to be rescued and restored? If not, there is a point in time where this might turn out to be sadly true, a tipping point or start of an avalanche where mitigation and restoration are no longer possible, not so much for the earth as such but for many life forms on earth, including us humans. Were that fateful day to arrive—and for all we currently know, it might not be very far in the future—then our procrastination, hesitation, indifference, partisanship, and delay would be shown to have had fatal consequences for our human species or at least for human civilization as we know and experience it today.

Nature writer and environmental forewarner Bill McKibben writes these ominous words in his *New Yorker* newsletter: "You would think that changes in the planet's climate would take a very long time and changes in human opinion and action could happen fast. You'd think that sentience would be an aid. But, instead, it appears that we are slow and that nature—

supercharged by our carbon—is fast as hell. Since the climate crisis isn't going to slow down, our only option is to speed up" (2021). McKibben's reflections are certainly sobering. We are experiencing today in inescapable ways the effects of global climate change, effects that began in the early days of the Industrial Revolution but that have reached an alarmingly accelerating rate, especially since the 1950s. The anomalous and frightening implication of this fact, as McKibben points out, is that changes in the earth's climate and ecosystems that formerly occurred with lumbering slowness over large stretches of time are happening so fast today that we humans, having recently become increasingly aware of them and rightly alarmed by them, are desperately in need of trying to find ways to counter them and bring them under control as quickly as possible. We need to do so rapidly enough to forestall and reverse their destructive consequences for all forms of life on the earth, including our own, before the consequences become irreversible and by then too late.

Symptoms of the change are current worldwide phenomena such as raging wildfires; rising heat waves; longer summers; more frequent and intense storms; changes in ocean temperature, acidity, and volume; melting glaciers and ice sheets; increasing droughts and desertifications; and dire effects of all of these things on the health and wellbeing of wildlife. In the meantime, we humans seem distressingly slow in responding in timely fashion to their urgency—even in many cases refusing to admit there is an emergency. Our institutions are equally sluggish in finding ways to acknowledge and meet their challenge. Our commitment to getting rid of destructive emissions into the atmosphere and pollutions of ground, groundwater, and oceans; our addiction to corporate profits and indifference to externalities in our industrial productions; the ponderous slowness of our ability to size up and do something about impending environmental disasters—pose the serious threat of human unwillingness to take seriously the threatening crisis whose indications are all around us.

Such indications pose the question: Are we up to the challenge? Or must we resign ourselves to the conclusion that we are not and that ruin will fall upon the earth and its ecosystems, ruin that will become increasingly real and irreversible for the generations that follow our own? We are creatures with remarkable teleological capacities, as I continue to emphasize in this book. But will we learn how to put them into practice soon enough to avert imminent global disaster—disaster not only for our own species but for innumerable other ones? The earth has deep resources and staying power, and will no doubt survive our rampant contemporary misuses of these resources, but our human civilization—at least as we take it for granted today—may not. The magnitude of the ecological problems that confront us today threatens to reduce us to a kind of despairing fatalism, a grim dread of what looks like inevitable disaster.

We can avoid approaching cataclysm and fatal erosion of confidence in our human ability to confront, mitigate, and reverse their threatening onset by putting our considerable, highly evolved intelligence, strength, and freedom of action into effect. Weakness of will is not an inherent trait of humankind. Nature has created us with the tools we need to cope with radical changes in our earthly environment, changes that we are bringing about by negligence, lack of appropriate attention, and failure to develop commonality of purpose and clear recognition of and responsibility for impending disaster.

The task of finding timely and effective ways of drawing on our collective strength is an extremely daunting one, but it is not impossible. We must not lose heart. Our habits can be changed, our laws improved, our practices redirected, and our institutions reformed and brought to bear on the urgent task of dealing with what is probably one of the greatest crises ever to confront humankind and other creatures of earth—a crisis that threatens to be similar to, if not on a par with, the five great extinction events of the earth's remote past.

Our fate is not determined. We are free. And in this fact lies hope for ourselves and for much of the fate of the earth in our time. But we need to get to work right away in a focused, intelligent, institutional, collective manner on the task if we are to avert the doleful consequences of neglecting for too long to attend to it.

Debates about the stout maintenance of individual freedoms, on the one hand, and a pressing need to have recourse to more collective, corporate strategies, on the other, should recede into the background because the only way to avert fatal erosion of individual freedom is to fail to have needed recourse to collective action. Isolated individuals cannot accomplish the hugely demanding task alone. But it is also true that individual contributions to the character and direction of more collective actions are desperately needed. Time should not be wasted in partisan bickering but be relentlessly devoted to the task at hand. At no time has the proper balance between individuals and groups needed more careful and concerted attention.

We must awaken to the powerful reality of our human freedom while there is still time—a freedom manifested in all the remarkable accomplishments of our cultural past. Our present situation is not hopeless, but it is deeply troubling. Our power to destroy by misuses of our freedom or failures to make prompt and necessary uses of it are by now amply evident. But so too is evidence of human freedom's power to do good and of its achievements of many remarkably good things in the face of formidable odds. No discussion of teleology should fail to take notice of either of these two facts.

In order to add more flesh or substance to the development of telic values that is the principal focus of this chapter, I turn next to discussion of what I regard as three commonplace miracles, things so commonplace as usually to be taken for granted and not acknowledged as the extraordinary things they really are when properly reflected on and attended to.

Three Commonplace Miracles

Three entirely natural miracles have made teleology possible, as I am defining and discussing it in this chapter and elsewhere in this book. I use the term *miracle* advisedly and etymologically as something truly wonderous and amazing (Latin, *miror, mirari*: "to marvel at") at least when we take the time to reflect on it. Such miracles are even more extraordinary in my view when we stop to think how commonplace or ubiquitous they are on the face of the earth. And all of them are miracles of material phenomena that do not require, in my view, creation or guidance by a separate divine spirit or spirits or by some kind of mind that is already and always immanent in the world. A miracle does not have to be inexplicable or supernatural in order to qualify as a miracle. The most impressive miracles are the natural ones.

These three miracles involve no mind-boggling, disturbingly unintelligible metaphysical dualisms such as that of a purely spiritual, transcendent, or even timeless God somehow creating and being intimately related to a temporal material world, or that of a separate mental substance somehow attached to a purely material body. Instead, the three involve only natural miracles of increasingly emergent complexity of organization and sophistication of functioning. The three miracles I have in mind are so-called ordinary matter, unconscious life, and conscious life. In the last two, as I continue to argue, there is teleology or goal-directed, purposive behavior, and in the third one this behavior becomes increasingly conscious and intentional, with its maximum level in human beings at the current stage of biological evolution on earth. The first miracle, once emergent and developed, provides the necessary basis for the other two.

Evolutionary emergence itself is not goal directed, but it has produced an abundance of living creatures that are such, namely, telic beings with telic values and ends. All of this was made possible by matter-energy interacting with time, and by time being recognized as the combination of varying degrees of continuity and novelty—of continuously emerging real possibilities that became a basis for the further emergence of new actualities. It is in the nature of nature that this process be what it is and what it has brought about. Behind the three miracles I am now indicating as such lies the master miracle of nature itself from which all else on earth and elsewhere in the present universe has emerged and continues to emerge.

As I noted in chapter 3, nature in my metaphysical perspective is the ultimate given, with its two primordials of matter-energy and time, and all else flows from and is sustained by this given. In chapter 2, I called brief attention to how or by what successive processes or stages ordinary matter, life, and conscious life have come into being. In chapter 1, I defended the emergentist, indeterminist, materialist teleology that constitutes for me the most convincing of the five interpretations of teleology I referred to there. What I am presently emphasizing is *how miraculous these three are*, despite the fact that they have required nothing greater (or lesser) than nature itself for their origination, development, and explanation.

If an adequate worldview requires awesome, deeply inspirational miracles at its heart, the view I am outlining here and discussing throughout this book presents miracles aplenty for our contemplation. A naturalistic account of teleological phenomena like the one I am describing is no less miraculous in the sense of that term I am now recommending than a supernaturalistic one. This claim should not be dismissed solely on the ground of its allegedly bland ordinariness or all too easily taken for granted familiarity but enthusiastically and regularly recognized for its miraculous, wondrous quality.

I am well aware that others call attention to their fervently felt need and cognitive requirement for supernatural explanations of nature and its telic phenomena. I respect such views and do not mean to dismiss their good-faith intentions out of hand. But for me, nature and its profuse intrinsic miracles are more than enough. Nothing further in the way of a supernatural origin and maintenance of nature or of ultimate rescue from its ambiguities and alleged deficiencies is needed. This claim holds true for the rampant number of teleological beings on earth, including those of our human species. All of us are at home here and must find ways to live peaceably, justly, and productively together.

Sources of Ultimate Authority

Where do the moral, religious, scientific, aesthetic, and political sensibilities, capacities, and values of human beings come from? What is their ultimate source and basis? My answer should be clear by now. They come from us as creatures of nature who are capable by nature of perceptive, intentional, rational, collectively deliberating thinking and behavior. These capabilities provide, in turn, abundant purposes, meanings, goals, and values for the living of our lives, individually and socially. No more ultimate authority is needed. Together with our nature as end-oriented and end-directed teleological beings goes the necessity of being responsive, responsible thinkers and actors in every area of our lives.

Morality requires empathetic relations to other humans as well as to all of the living creatures of earth. There have long been and are today tragic consequences of avoiding or foolishly trying to avoid morally responsible relationships with one another. The Holocaust of the Second World War and the other horrible atrocities, terrible destructions, and rampant injustices of that war are examples. The presently looming ecological crisis is another. The at least relatively successful adaptations of humans to their natural and social environments in the past make perspicuously evident the continuing need for discovery, development, and enactment of workable moral precepts, principles, and relationships. We have no other real option than that of getting along with one another as humans and with the other creatures of the earth, and finding ways to flourish together.

Religion requires recognition of the sacred character of the earth and all that it contains. This recognition elicits heartfelt responsiveness to the sacred, cultivation of intense feelings of its presence, and the response of one's inner being to its reality, presence, and demand throughout the world and in every aspect of human life. Religious feeling, thought, and commitment provide context and motivation for moral sensitivity and moral living, as well as awakening us to the wonders of the world and of ourselves as a part of the world.

Art, in the forms of music, dance, sculpture, painting, architecture, and the like, calls our attention to the pervasive beauty and wonder of the earth in microbe, bug, fish, animal, person, tree, flower, mountain, valley, sea, and sky—as well as in the networks of their relations to one another. Art also helps to make us aware in depths of empathetic feeling of the sorrowful and tragic dimensions of life—sensitizing us to ugliness and despair as well as to beauty and joy. In this way it makes essential contributions to both our moral and our religious sensibilities.

Science grows out of our attempts and needs to understand the processes of nature and our role within those processes, and to do so with the imaginative and analytical minds that are our gifts of nature as human beings—the same minds that are brought into play in many other dimensions of our experiences and cultures. There are crucial facts to be discovered and truths to be known, or at least to be better known, in the domain of science. Knowledge of them is necessary if we are to be responsible citizens of the community of creatures and their respective domains on earth. We dare not ignore patient researchers and responsible experts in the fields of science, particularly in areas of ecological concern.

Civic, social, and political principles and precepts stem from this same twofold source, our natural environment and our need to live peaceably, productively, and justly with one another as humans and with the other creatures of earth and with respect for the natural environments that render their lives and ours possible. I need no more ultimate sources and explanations than these, although others feel an urgent need to have recourse to their origins and maintenances by something believed to be even more ultimate, such as God or the gods, or in some sort of primordial, panpsychistic teleology.

For me, the buck stops with us and with our relations to the natural order as we experience it and have come to understand it on earth. Here is the ultimate authority and responsibility, whether for good or ill. We must, after all, be the interpreters, appropriators, and appliers of what we may take to be the will and purpose of a God, a sacred text, a set of legal precepts, and so on. Merely to parrot such things is not earnestly or meaningfully to incorporate them into our everyday lives.

But what of the need for salvation? Isn't that what religion is all about? Where does it come from, if not from God or some kind of supernatural realm beyond this world? It comes, in my view, from the depths of nature experienced and revered as hallowed ground. And its effect is not some kind of transport into another, nonnatural world but profound, grateful awareness of our being truly at home here in the natural world. Cultivation of this awareness is the work of a lifetime and not at all easy to come by. This is the central teaching of some religious outlooks such as Daoism and at least some versions of pantheism, and all or almost all religions stress it to a significant extent because the sacred or holy is said by them to reside in the depths of things as we experience them here on earth, and that in attunement with these depths we discover the secrets of salvation. Even the most radical kind of theism typically speaks of God as both immanent and transcendent as their sustainer and creator. To discover the miracles of everyday life is also, then, to discover the presence of the sacred in every aspect of our lives.

At this point we need to remind ourselves that recourse to God as the ultimate source and explanation of everything else in nature is an *interpretation*, and a debatable one at that, as the history of religions clearly shows. We cannot escape the role of human interpreters in all of the domains I have mentioned—the religious one inescapably included. *There is no such thing as uninterpreted authority.* We humans are the final interpreters, focusing our own interpretations on the interpretations provided for us by the great religious founders, prophets, and teachers of human history. When they claim to speak of revelations given to them by God, we have to interpret and accept these claims as true if we decide to allow them to constitute the basis of our conception, experience, and promise of salvation. The hand of the human hangs heavily over any and all claims about ultimate religious truths.

This is not to brand such claims as false, indefensible, or undependable. It is only to recognize their defeasible character, a character made evident by the differences—and in some cases, profound differences—among the religions of the world. To choose one religious vision over others is to engage in an act of fallible interpretation. To reject them all is also an act, or a series of acts, of interpretation.

I readily admit and subscribe to the fallibility of my own faith stance of religious naturalism that runs explicitly and implicitly through the discussions of this book. Disagreements about fundamental existential choices, interpretations, and values are probably inevitable, and we continue to have much to learn from the various forms of them in our conversations with one another—religious and secular persons alike. But in the final analysis, the buck of interpretation begins and ends with each of us as goal-oriented, truth-seeking, and value-seeking interpreters. We cannot escape the burden, invitation, and promise of this unavoidable fact. And as for the abundant values of many different sorts recognized and encountered in nature, they are all derived from the potencies and processes of nature and are not bestowed upon nature from somewhere else or by some source outside itself. This statement is consistent not only with the standpoint of religious naturalism but also with the entirely immanental, purely internal brand of teleology I am arguing for in this chapter. We need look nowhere else for their fully adequate sanction and support.

Conclusion

In this chapter, I have stressed the critical role of chance or contingency, along with causality, in explaining the presence of natural values throughout the earth. All such values are emergent rather than primordial or derivative from outside of nature, and the whole of nature itself throughout our vast present universe is an object of supreme value. *Nature natured*, with all of its valuative aspects and dimensions, is the product of *nature naturing*, and no dualistic interpretation of these two terms is sanctioned or intended. The two go necessarily together and cannot be separately conceived.

Nature never stands or ever has stood completely still, in other words. It is endlessly dynamic or processive, and its prescriptive values or ends are as much the outcomes of its internal processes as are its more descriptive factual aspects. Our present universe has come into being partly on the basis of an earlier one, and that one on another one, back into endless time. Time itself is endlessly creative of both fact and value as it interacts with matter-energy.

I put special emphasis in this chapter on three fundamental types of value, the fate of the earth and its nonhuman creatures, the fate of humans, and the prospect of human freedom and hope. And I discussed the crucial importance of the proper and beneficial exercise of human freedom for the sake of the future of the earth's ecosystems and of our own flourishing and survival as necessarily dependent parts of these systems.

Our freedom is exceptional among the creatures of earth, and for that reason its forward-looking, compassionate, rational exercise is vitally important for their sakes as well as for our own. As creatures of nature with exceptional gifts, we humans are exceptionally responsible for the future of the earth. We need to take this responsibility seriously to heart as we contemplate our central role in the current ecological crisis.

We are by nature integral participants in nature naturing, important agents of its creativity and of our own and the earth's hope. Fate is not something to be resignedly accepted. Subject to our freedom as the fate of much of the earth and of ourselves as creatures of earth undeniably is, its fate is by virtue of that fact also subject to our realistic—but also strongly envisioned and intended—effort and hope. Values make a difference, and this species of value can make a decisive difference for our planet's future. Teleology, values, and the shape of the future are bound inseparably together. The ecological situation today is an urgent one, not one to be dithered away or repeatedly postponed. Time is of the essence for this exceedingly dangerous situation.

The three *commonplace* but also *remarkable miracles* of the evolution of ordinary matter, of life, and of conscious life on earth have also been given prominent attention in this chapter. I have argued that none of the three requires recourse to something outside nature or to some kind of primordial mind resident in nature from the outset. All three have been created and evolved by processes immanent within nature. In my mind, they are all the more astonishing and inspiring in view of this account of their origin and status.

Finally, I gave particular attention to moral, religious, artistic, scientific, and civic values that are regularly encountered and entrenched in human life and have such critical roles to play in it. I argued that all of them are natural in their character and not derivative from some other source than nature. I insisted that our salvation and the radical resolution of the earth's present ecological dangers depend on its immanent resources, and especially on the long overdue ameliorative, restorative, and just actions of us humans.

I also contended that claims about each of these areas of thought and attention result from acts of interpretation and that there is no such thing as either an uninterpreted fact or an uninterpreted value. This is true whether we regard them as immanent aspects of our experiences of nature or as somehow conferred upon nature from without. In this chapter, I interpret both their character and their status as entirely natural or immanent. Those who interpret the case differently have interpretations different from my own. But none of us is entitled to appeal to something alleged to lie beyond the fallibilities and differences of our best efforts of interpretation and understanding.

Chapter Five

Panpsychism and Emergent Novelty

> Proponents of emergence theory emphasize the unpredictability of
> higher-level phenomena in order to safeguard the irreducibility and
> reality of such phenomena. If they were predictable, then it would be
> possible to reduce their ontological structure and causal capacities to
> their underlying basic structure. Although this resistance to reductionism
> is understandable, it makes higher-level phenomena, such as teleological
> properties, *sui generis* and unexplainable.
>
> —Mikael Leidenhag (2019: 13)

A critic of the emergentist explanation of teleological phenomena defended
in this book is Swedish scholar Mikael Leidenhag. He defends a version
of *panpsychism* and argues, as the epigraph to this chapter indicates, that
the *emergentism* I am relying on so far in this book to account for teleology or end-directed phenomena is "unexplainable." He reasons in part
that teleological phenomena must be sui generis in any emergentist view,
meaning that they cannot successfully be shown to be truly natural, thus
implying a strikingly incoherent and thus unexplainable *dualism* of natural
phenomena, on the one hand, and teleological ones, on the other (2019:
14–15). Although Leidenhag is willing to say that the *sophistication* of mind
evolves, he thinks that the separate *existence* of mind is constant, underived,
and operative throughout.

In this chapter, I want to explore in detail some of Leidenhag's grounds
for arguing in this way and to show that these grounds do not take sufficiently
into account or tend to misconstrue the kinds of reasoning on which the

emergentist view can be based and defended, at least so far as my conception of it is concerned. Although I disagree with Leidenhag in this regard, I also commend his endeavor to critically analyze the crucial issue of teleology, both in the article from which this chapter's epigraph is taken and in his wide-ranging monograph entitled *Naturalizing God? A Critical Evaluation of Religious Naturalism*, published in 2021. My disagreements with him do not mean that I lack appreciation for his efforts to show that emergentism is mistaken. These efforts, and the logic of his defense of panpsychism they help to bring to light, not only enable me better to understand his view. The need for responses to his defense on my part have also helped me to think more clearly about and to give expression to what I regard as the logic of the counterview I espouse. When the different logics of emergentism and panpsychism are exposed in this manner, each of us can be better equipped to see just what it is we are disagreeing about. Each can do a commendable service to the other in this way.

Leidenhag's criticism of religious naturalism in both his article and in his book is to a large degree a criticism of emergentism that sets the stage for his own defense of panpsychism—a defense he believes to be required in order to save religious naturalism from fatal incoherence when it is based on some version of emergentism, as it frequently and typically is. My focus in this chapter is not on religious naturalism as such but on a defense of emergentism and criticism of panpsychism as an alternative to emergentism. I engage in this task by responding to some of the particular arguments against emergentism that Leidenhag develops with arguments critical of his defenses of panpsychism. The present chapter is intended to add additional depth and strength to my interpretations of teleology that constitute the basic concern of this book.

By my count, the defense of panpsychism and its accompanying critique of emergentism, contained in Leidenhag's 2019 article and in chapter 8 of his 2019 book subtitled "Panpsychism," amounts to eleven separate arguments. Eight of these arguments are intended to expose basic weaknesses or elements of fundamental untenability or unintelligibility in emergentism, while the remaining three are forthright defenses of panpsychism in the face of directed attacks on its credibility. I shall not focus on each of these argument topics separately but shall incorporate aspects of them into a digest of what I take to be the logic of the arguments, and present and defend emergentism by elucidating its own logic and showing why I think emergentism makes more sense as an explanation for teleological phenomena.

My digest lists five main classes of argument presented by Leidenhag in his article and in chapter 8 of his book: an incomprehensible origination of mind from mere matter, given the incompatibility of mind with mere matter; the indefensibility of thinking that telic norms could arise solely from allegedly original facts; the argument that emergentism entails an incoherent mind-body dualism; the allegation that panpsychism is implicit in emergentist accounts of the origin of mind and its teleological capacities; and Leidenhag's contention that panpsychism is a genuine and convincing explanation of teleological phenomena, not an arbitrarily posited, simply named, or groundlessly projected one. I shall present what I regard as convincing responses to each of these five classes of argument in turn. In this manner, I will have developed additional defenses of my emergentist view of the origins and developments of mental and teleological phenomena on earth.

Incomprehensible Origination of Mind from Matter

The first argument claims as incomprehensible the idea that mind could evolve from matter, and therefore that mind must be a primordial and nonderivative factor in nature. The steady progress toward the origins and developments of mind alleged by emergentism would be inexplicable without acceptance of the immanence of mind in all of nature from the very outset. So in addition to the two primordial factors I assume for nature, namely, matter-energy and time, Leidenhag contends that we must add some sort of primordial mind or indwelt mental tendency in nature from the outset to explain the rise of mental phenomena. Mind, then, does not evolve. It is a fundamental feature of nature at all times and in all places.

This argument makes two assumptions that must be challenged. The first one concerns its implicit conception of matter, and the second one concerns its apparent notion of time. The concept of matter that Leidenhag seems to assume is that it is something fixed and unchangeable, always and forever what it is and must be conceived to be. As such, it has nothing mental connected with it. This conception would be consistent with a Newtonian view of matter, but it is hardly consistent with the contemporary scientific view of it.

In the contemporary view, matter-energy is astoundingly *protean*, *volatile*, and *processive* rather than fixed in its nature. It is a form of energy, and it has evolved over time from the Big Bang explosion, with its rain of neutrons, electrons, positrons, photons, and neutrons; to the four forces of electromagnetism, the strong nuclear force, the weak force of neutron decay, and gravity; from initial hydrogen atoms to types of atoms exceeding by today's count well over one hundred in number; to innumerable kinds of molecules made up of such atoms; and thence to the countless forms of matter such as those we experience and encounter today. It should be emphasized here that ordinary matter is itself the outcome of a kind of emergent evolution. Included in the innumerable forms of matter are the millions of species of *living* matter, some now extinct and others existing on earth today.

With the origination of life there have also originated the three most basic traits of mind depicted by Evan Thompson, that is, autopoiesis, sentience, and purposiveness. And from this earlier basis more complex kinds of mind have steadily emerged, including earlier and later stages of *conscious* mind. Matter has in these ways shown itself to be relentlessly creative and fecund. Why should we assume with Leidenhag that it is incapable of giving rise to mind and various stages or levels of mind as part of its fecundity?

Newton's conception of matter was something fixed, mechanical, and forever the same. Evolution does not enter into his view, and his atoms are quite different from the atoms of today, given that they are unresolvable into more fundamental and quite active constituents and that they exhibit no aspects of indeterminacy or chance such as would be required for an interpretation of the evolving nature of matter. As I read him, this first class of Leidenhag's arguments seems to have something like Newtonian matter in mind with its sharp dichotomization of matter and mind. It is more akin to Cartesian dualism than to contemporary emergentism.

What I also detect as a deficiency in this first class of Leidenhag's arguments against an emergentist conception of mind is a radical underestimation and overlooking of the demonstrable creative power of *time*. Time makes a difference, and it often makes radical differences, not only in the origins and developments of ordinary matter, stars, galaxies, planets, and planetary systems, but even of the origin of a universe such as the one we humans presently inhabit. The flow of time is not just continuous. It is also changing. Time combines, at every stage of its ceaseless flowing, aspects of continuity and novelty. It is this combination that makes time endlessly creative, and this creativity is reflected in cosmic, terrestrial, biological, and cultural evolution. All creation, and indeed all kinds of change, are transformations of something in previous existence. There is no such thing as absolute, de novo change, or *creatio ex nihilo*. And the flow of time itself, by this reasoning, has no beginning or ending. Creativity also includes destruction, as aspects of the old are necessarily left behind in order for the new to emerge.

The creative powers of time seem to me to be incontestable. If so, why should we think, as Leidenhag seems to, that the emergence of mind from matter is something *impossible to conceive* as taking place over vast stretches of time? Taking the creative powers of time seriously and recognizing the radical changes they have brought about over the 13.8-billion-year history of the present universe makes it entirely conceivable that mind and the telic and other powers of mind could have come into being as revelations of latent potentialities of matter-energy were made progressively actual over time. They were made actual by means of the creative novelty contained in the very notion of time as the inexorable combination of continuity and novelty.

Given this combination, the possibilities of something such as matter-energy are not confined to any given time but continue to emerge over time. Life and its accompanying mental capacities—at first primitive but gradually more sophisticated—were admittedly not possible at the time of the Big Bang, at least not then as a *real* possibility. But they became increasingly possible with the extensive passage of time. The same analysis holds for the emergence of material beings with increasing capacity for consciously intended kinds of behavior. We may not be capable at present of a complete understanding of how such things have happened, but their happening in this manner is neither impossible nor completely incomprehensible, as shown by the history of emerging, increasingly complex forms of matter and material beings on earth to which I am calling attention in this section.

Partial understanding is still understanding. It does not amount to the kind of complete incomprehensibility Leidenhag seems to assume and to urge us to assume in assenting to the kind of argument against the emergentist teleology and philosophy of mind under consideration here. Mind is not incompatible with matter in the latter perspective. It is crucially dependent on matter. Material minds are not like married bachelors. These two are not contradictory concepts but entirely consistent ones. Apart from material systems of some sort, there would be no such things as the functions of minds. Matter is historically prior to mind. This is the conclusion to which the reasoning of this section leads. It makes unnecessary the primordial panpsychism Leidenhag champions.

Telic Norms Cannot Arise Solely from Original Facts

Leidenhag's insistence that telic norms or values cannot arise solely from original facts seems to me to imply tacit agreement with something akin to David Hume's alleged "is-ought" fallacy or with George Edward Moore's alleged "naturalistic fallacy," to both of which I made brief mention in a note to chapter 3. But as I indicated in that chapter, I do not believe that values need be inferred from mere facts. Facts can occasion or invite normative responses, but these responses are not reducible to or mistakenly inferred from the related bare facts. Norms can be discovered and described in nature just as facts can. Nature is replete with implicit values or norms awaiting recognition and discovery, as I argued at length in that chapter. But we can be mistaken in assertions about value, just as we can be mistaken about assertions regarding fact.

I do not subscribe to anything like the untenable idea that the mere act of valuing something or other automatically converts it into a recognizable or defensible value. Ascriptions of value can be meaningfully debated, just as can ascriptions of fact. But I do believe that factors such as the successful evolutionary adaptations of organisms to their natural environments disclose aspects of value, and of adequately confirmed value, in those environments. Values are admittedly different from facts, but both are interpretations of natural phenomena that may be open to challenge as well as amenable to defense.

Furthermore, recognitions or discoveries of values do not imply to me some sort of original or primordial mind or teleology in nature. Such recognitions and discoveries do not entail panpsychism. What they do require as their necessary and prior basis is the *evolution* of minds because neither facts nor values can be acknowledged or claimed as such apart from the evolutions of minds of some sort, including the earliest kinds of mentality resultant from biological evolution. Facts and values exist as such in relation to minds, and neither is discernible apart from minds. So the evolution of minds and of teleological phenomena of all kinds is essential for either discrete facts or discernible values to exist or be recognizable as such. Facts and values alike exist in their relations to minds capable of detecting, relating to, and making use of them as such. These minds are emergent products of evolution.

I listed in the preceding section many different kinds of material phenomena that have stemmed from the time of the Big Bang. These phenomena, after themselves originating from and then undergoing long processes of evolution, organization, and change, eventually gave rise to innumerable kinds of living bodies capable of varying kinds and degrees of mentality. This view of things shows a priority of materiality to relatively late-arriving mentality. It does not reveal a primordiality of mind. The view is also the considered conclusion of the great majority of today's scientists, based on careful formulations of theoretical hypotheses and empirical tests of these hypotheses that give impressive support to the now common scientific beliefs about the evolutionary past.

This now commonly accepted view runs counter to a claimed original presence of mind in the evolving universe. Mind is regarded as derivative, and I think properly so. Only matter-energy and time need to be assumed as primordial, and under the influences of temporal creativity and change matter-energy has undergone many fundamental alterations, including the emergences of more and more complex living forms and systems of matter capable of discerning with increasing levels of mental prowess and attention both facts and values critical for their flourishing and survival. Once evolved as human beings, such material forms of life show themselves to be capable of discerning, analyzing, and defending a current pervasive presence of natural values as well as natural facts, as I do—or of formulating and defending a version of panpsychism, as Leidenhag does. The principal difference between us is that he sees mind as still another kind of underived, unevolved, necessary primordial principle, while I see mental phenomena as originating and becoming increasingly present only with the gradual evolution of material forms of life over vast expanses of time.

Emergentism Entails Indefensible Mind-Body Dualism

Leidenhag contends that mental and teleological properties are incompatible with material ones, and thus that there is no way in which mind could emerge from and be produced by matter. For him, the two are different orders of being. No matter how complex the organizations and types of matter might have become over evolutionary time, they could not have produced mind. But if we reason, as Even Thompson does and as I do, that life and some sort and degree of mind are necessarily combined, no matter how minimal the kind of mind involved, then we would also have to reject the whole idea of biological evolution. In other words, we would have to reject the origination of not only mind from matter, but life itself as the outcome of an emergent or evolutionary process.

We would also have to conclude, at least in my judgment, that it would make no sense to think that material bodies can somehow give support to minds or allow minds to have the effects on material bodies we routinely observe them to have. Leidenhag's incompatibility claim seems to make impossible any kinds of interaction between mind and body and to imply an incoherent type of Cartesian dualism. This is a heavy price to pay in order to defend panpsychism. I do not see how it is possible to argue for a radical distinction between mind and body in order to defend the primordiality and underivability of mind from matter, on the one hand, and continue to assume the ongoing interaction of the two, on the other. If mind is to affect matter, and matter to affect mind, as we observe them to do day by day, then they cannot be incompatible orders of being.

If it is true that in the earliest phases of the evolution of material beings there were no minds—as I believe to have been the case—this fact does not require that we conceive of mind as already present in nature in order to account for its eventual evolution. By this reasoning, instead of mind being created by matter, and specifically by living matter, mind was *always there* awaiting manifestation and expression by material forms of life capable of giving it support and expression.

The problem with this view, however, is that of how any kind of matter, regardless of how complex its organization, could have any bearing on the manifestation of an earlier latent mind, if mind and matter are incompatible with one another as distinct orders of being. The more credible view would seem to me to be the idea that a proper kind and sufficiency of material organization—and especially those kinds already involving some kind of neuronal system—produces mental properties, functions, and modes of behavior. In this scenario, which I believe to be conceptually much more likely, bodies produce minds with ascending evolutionary phases of material organization, and minds are functions of particular kinds of organized matter.

If, on the other hand, matter and mind are incompatible orders of being, panpsychism becomes irrelevant to anything that takes place or can take place in the material world. Mind and matter, in this event, can have nothing to do with one another, which is an empirically preposterous position. The only possible solution to this position, it would seem, is some sort of mind-body *parallelism* where the two act in concert with seeming but illusionary interactions, without either having real effects on the other. This conclusion is not nearly as tenable as the contention that minds are functions of living bodies.

We do not today fully understand how matter can produce mind, and especially the qualitative, phenomenal aspects of mind familiar to us in our daily lives as humans, but it seems clear that matter and mind are closely connected with one another instead of being incompatible with one another. The defense of panpsychism that turns on the thesis of their incompatibility is not only vulnerable to the kind of fundamental objection to it I am mounting here; it also seems to me to be fatal to panpsychism itself. This is so because panpsychism is endorsed in the first place to account not only for mental phenomena in the world, including teleological, commonly witnessed, and routine goal-oriented behaviors, but also for the mind-body interactions required for those phenomena and behaviors to have their commonly observed impacts and outcomes in the world. If mind and matter are incompatible, then panpsychism as an explanatory stratagem goes by the board.

Mind and matter are *admittedly different* from one another, given that matter without mind is regularly experienced and entirely conceivable, whereas mind without matter is extremely difficult, if not impossible, to conceive—at least given the character of the natural world as we regularly encounter and experience it. But mind is not *so* different from matter as to prevent evolved material bodies from producing and sustaining minds or to render inconceivable the commonly experienced interactions of these two aspects of the world. The two are also obviously closely related to one another, else I would not be capable of writing this sentence on my computer, having it eventually published as part of a bound or digital book, and by these physical actions and means communicating, through your physical eyes and nervous system, an aspect of my mind to an aspect of yours.

Panpsychism as Implicit in Any Kind of Emergentism

Leidenhag defends his panpsychist outlook in part with the argument that the emergence of life, as well as the later emergence of life forms capable of various levels of consciousness, presuppose the presence of some sort of experience or mindlike, phenomenal properties in all of nature or all of reality. All entities, according to this view, gain their capability of interacting with one another by a kind of *information processing* or even by what can rightly be termed *semiosis*. Panpsychism can therefore also be understood as *pansemiosis*. Emergence from nonlife to life, and from nonconscious to conscious forms of life, is made possible and explicable, therefore, only if we assume to be built into all of reality from the very outset—whether living or nonliving—a distinctively mental character, quality, or capability. This mental factor does not *emerge* with complex levels of material organization. It is already there, and were it not, the emergence of life from nonlife, and the emergence of conscious mind from nonconscious mind, could not occur. Mind, therefore, is primordial rather than derivative.

The problem with this kind of argument, as I see it, is at least twofold. The first problem is that it confuses key metaphors with literal conceptions. The second one is that it makes mind such a broad category that it encompasses any kind of causal interaction or relationship. Terms like *information* and *semiosis* lose their more literal meanings when applied to reality at its most basic levels. To speak of all cause-effect relationships as literal communications of *information* or as literally *signaling* by some sort of implicit *sign system* to their effects is to deprive these terms of their original, more usual kinds of literal meaning. Metaphors are certainly useful and may often prove to be indispensable, but they should not be misused or allowed to mislead our thought. And when used as basic terms in an important system of thought such as *information* theory and *biosemiosis* theory, which Leidenhag draws upon in support of panpsychism, we should be constantly aware of their metaphorical character.

A digital computer can metaphorically be referred to as an *information system* or as having the capability of *conveying information* from one human being to another. But in the absence of human beings who created and make use of this machine for such a purpose, it is nothing more than a sophisticated electronic system. What it stores is not literally memory, and what it processes are not mental phenomena but physical ones. Apart from its mental creators and interpreters, there would be no literal communication of information or meaningful interpretation of signs. Signs become *significant* only in this manner. And mind comes into being only when sufficiently complex systems have evolved to make *life* and its accompanying mental processes possible. The metaphorical uses of such terms as *information*, *memory*, *sign*, *signal*, *communication*, and the like are certainly useful in many contexts. But confusion of their metaphorical uses with literal ones can lead us astray. This confusion takes place, in my view, with the kind of argument under discussion in this section.

What Leidenhag seems systematically to overlook in his defenses of panpsychism is the crucial role of *time*. I made this point earlier in this chapter, but it is worth reiterating here. Time often works slowly and by incremental stages to bring genuinely new, unprecedented things into being. They were not already there, even in germ, until levels of real possibility for their subsequent emergence as actualities have emerged.

In other words, contained in the proximal and distant past are possibilities that the course of time allows to become actual. These are real, not pure, possibilities. No realm of pure possibility is required. Seeing one color red, a painter can imagine a new version of red not yet mixed on the painter's palette or maybe on any other painter's palette. A composer or singer, by responding consciously or unconsciously to certain songs or melodies from the past, can come up with a new kind of music called the blues. Two bicycle makers and self-taught engineers can watch gulls soaring and imagine on that basis the possibility of making a powered, controllable airplane. If birds do it, perhaps we humans can find a way to do it as well!

There is no baby without a previous fetus, to cite further examples. There is no fetus without a zygote. There is no zygote without the union of sperm and egg. And there is no union of sperm and egg without the combination of male and female genes. There would be no such things as male and female human beings or their respective genetic makeups without complex types of material organization that came into existence long ago by the interworkings of causal continuity and chance, that is, by the influences of the past and opportunities posed by those influences for new realizations of the future. Time makes things new only by its ability to transform older things. And among these transformative outcomes are living and then conscious forms of matter.

We can say that matter-energy, in concert with enormous spans of time, had the potentiality to create life from the outset. But this is to speak very abstractly and from the perspective of present ways of reasoning and understanding. It is to ignore by a kind of linguistic sleight of hand what took ages of change and development to make *really* possible. The fact that mind is present today does not imply—to say nothing of entail—that it has always been present in some manner, and that only this assumption can account for its emergence at later stages of biological evolution. The genuinely creative powers of time should not be forgotten or ignored. Panpsychism looks to me like some sort of timeless view of what is possible in the areas of mind and conscious mind. We commonly take for granted today the idea that such creatures as bacteria, plants, spiders, chimpanzees, and humans did not always exist. Why must we assume that mind has always existed in some primordial manner? If we are able to imagine the emergence of life, why not mind as well—mind as a distinctive property, albeit a minimal one in the earliest stages of evolution—of all emergent forms of life?

Panpsychism Not an Arbitrarily Posited Solution

As Leidenhag points out in one part of the eighth chapter of his book, panpsychism is sometimes branded as an arbitrary, merely posited, or penciled-in solution to the problem of why mind, and especially conscious mind, is conspicuously present on earth. If viewed as such, he notes, it would be a meaningless, empty, unhelpful proposed solution to a difficult problem. I give him credit for developing a defense of panpsychism that is much more sophisticated and worthy of consideration than this critical claim allows. Did I not regard it in this way, I would hardly have expended the effort to develop the arguments of this chapter against panpsychism.

There is thus some truth in this fifth class of his arguments against emergentism. There is still much that we do not understand about the relations of matter to mind, and this fact lends some credence to the panpsychist position, showing that it is not just an arbitrary allegation made in defense of the position. Instead, it is a serious attempt to account for the presence of mental phenomena in the world. However, assuming and arguing that mind must be primordial rather than derivative from something more fundamental than mind itself seems to me to be at bottom and in some ways to be too *facile* as a proposed solution to a formidable problem. It can border at times on question-begging.

More basically, and this is what my counterarguments are intended to disclose, I believe such arguments to be wholly *unnecessary* when another, more plausible explanation for mind's presence on earth is readily available, namely, the emergentist argument I am explicating and defending in this chapter and throughout this book. This claim is especially cogent, in my view, given the responses to the other four classes of Leidenhag's arguments in defense of panpsychism I am presenting in this chapter, as well as with my arguments elsewhere in this book.

Theism, Religion, and Panpsychism

I want now to direct attention away from Leidenhag's five arguments against emergentism and in support of panpsychism to take note of another aspect of his thought. In chapter 7 of his book Leidenhag discusses three types of what he refers to as *theism* (traditional theism, panentheism, and pantheism) in order to attend to their relations to religious naturalism. His discussion in this chapter brings to my mind what I take to be one of the strong motives behind panpsychism in some quarters, as the latter may be conceived and argued for today. This motive, with its focus on some kind of God, can be understood as the strong desire to give credence to the idea that a primordial divine mind lies behind and is made manifest in natural phenomena such as the marvels and wonders of nature and especially in its creatures that are capable of mental and teleological modes of behavior. Special attention can be called in this regard to the conscious mental capabilities of humans as natural beings.

The immanence of God in all of nature to which commitment is given in these three forms of theism implies a primordial immanence of mind in all of nature. Such a view can also be said to evidence an underlying divine purpose of the world as a whole, in keeping with the idea that the world everywhere expresses the purposeful presence and activity of an immanently creative and sustaining God. This view is notably a panpsychist one.

The creative, sustaining, and purposeful mind of God is, according to such theistic views, continuously at work in the world, and it provides an ultimate explanation for mental and teleological phenomena in the world. I think that an implicit superiority and primordial originative power of the *mental* in contrast with the *physical* is also frequently part of such a view. Care must be taken to provide frank disclosure of such theistic assumptions when they are present in order to avoid a version of panpsychism that could amount, in the final analysis, to question-begging if the crucial theistic assumptions behind it have not been brought frankly and clearly to light.

As a religious naturalist of one kind, I do not believe in God, find persuasive evidence of the presence of God throughout nature, or regard nature as a creation of God. I do not hold that such a being or an abiding presence as God is impossible, nor do I even want to lay claim here to its improbability. But I do not find belief in God to be necessary in view of the availability of the emergentist way of thinking as an alternative for accounting for and explaining life and mind. I detect innumerable manifestations of *the sacred* in our human experiences of the wonders of nature and see no demand to *personify* the sacred in terms of some conception of God.

I called attention to what I regard as some of the most notable of these manifestations in chapter 3. But wondrous as they are, I do not regard them as revealing a personal God (traditional theism), a God within which all other reality is somehow contained (panentheism), or a God who is immanent throughout nature (pantheism). So I do not subscribe to or find convincing any such appeals to God as putative supports for panpsychism.

Leidenhag does not himself explicitly defend what he calls the three forms of theism in the seventh chapter of his book, but his discussion identifies what I believe to be a major current incentive for endorsing some sort of panpsychism. For me, nature is the sufficient focus of a powerful, lively, and quite adequate religious faith. There is no need for God or for talk about God. The immanent, pervasive sacredness of nature is enough. But I can see why panpsychism, with its belief in the original and under-ived character of mind, would be an attractive option for those of theistic persuasion. And I can understand the emotional and conceptual appeal of believing that nature has some fundamental kinds of immanent, ever-present, overarching purpose or purposes, meaning or meanings, given to it by a creator God that can guide and sustain us in the living of our lives.

This prospect is overridden, made unnecessary, and made unpersuasive for me by the immanent purposes, values, and meanings created and brought to our reverent attention by emergent evolution and by the creative powers of time as these powers interact and work ceaseless wonders with protean matter-energy over eons of this universe's history. It is significant to me that even in the biblical book of Genesis it takes *time* for God to create life and then human life. Everything does not spring into existence all at once. It's a matter of "days," but who knows with defensible surety how long these mythical days were conceived to be by those who finally penned this ancient and truly remarkable biblical book?

Before leaving the topic of belief in God and its relation to panpsychism, I want to comment briefly on the main title of Leidenhag's book: *Naturalizing God.* He seems to be implying with this title the idea that religious naturalism in all of its forms—or at least the ones he alludes to or has in mind in the writing of his book—amount to making God identical with nature. But religious naturalism as I understand it need assign no role to God or to the concept of God. It does not try to "naturalize" God but boldly puts nature in the place of God. It insists that *nature itself* is the most appropriate, adequate, and fulfilling focus of religious faith and commitment.

Nature for religious naturalism is inexhaustibly sacred, as I argued in chapter 3, but its sacredness does not require reference to God in any one of the three senses of theism Leidenhag talks about in the seventh chapter of his book, namely, traditional theism, panentheism, or pantheism. Religious naturalism in some of the most familiar of its forms is frankly *atheistic* but also takes strong issue with the negative connotations of this term, familiar in frequent but careless Western discourse, conceptualization, and usage. The upshot of these ruminations on the title of Leidenhag's book is that there seems to be an unspoken assumption he is making in the main title of his book and perhaps tacitly in some if not much of the writing of it, namely, that religion always has to involve some conception of God. In saying this, I am led further to wonder how much of Leidenhag's attraction to panpsychism in his article and book is informed by commitment, whether consciously or unconsciously, to belief in a primordially creative and sustaining *mind of God.*

If the assumption that religion always and everywhere requires belief in God were true—and it demonstrably is not—then the *atheism* of some forms of religious naturalism, including the one I myself happen to espouse, would be synonymous with the absence of religious faith and with rejection of all beliefs and practices that give meaningful expression to religious faith—which it emphatically is not. Religious naturalism is deeply religious but is such without belief or faith in God. Its faith, trust, hope, and commitment are in the inspiring, demanding, and assuring powers of nature. It is a naturalizing of *religion*, not a naturalizing of *God*. Some of the *functions* of God commonly associated with God in the West are attributed to nature by religious naturalism, but it does not grant to theism its central conviction of the fundamental metaphysical (or ontological) status and central religious role of some sort of God.

The unqualified identification of the whole of nature with *God*, as in another form of pantheism, would best be reinterpreted as viewing all of nature as *sacred*, the view I heartily espouse. To call nature *God* is confusing, misleading, and unnecessary. It is confusing because it conjures up implications, deeply rooted in the West and elsewhere, of divine *personality*, which it need not intend. It is misleading because the term *God* strongly implies a *distinct divine Being* conceived as the transcendent creator and sustainer of nature rather than being identical with nature. And it is unnecessary because it avows an *identity* of nature with God. If this is so, then why not just speak of *nature* and leave *God* out of the picture?

Pantheism in this event turns out to be nothing more than, or nothing different from, *pan-naturalism*: nature is not only through-and-through *sacred*; nature is *all that there is*. Reference to *Theos* or *God* is no longer required. Since *pantheism* so construed is nothing other than *religious naturalism*, the former term should be set aside as both superfluous and misleading. Interested readers can consult religious philosopher Demian Wheeler's helpful diagram portraying in four quadrants optional treatments of this issue (Wheeler 2018: 107).

I make these comments and those throughout my book, not in the spirit of a pitched battle with Leidenhag as an implacable foe, but in the spirit of critical but also constructive dialogue with a worthy dialogue partner. I do so in the hope that the two of us can better understand and learn from one another, and that others may also find instruction in pondering our similarities as well as our differences regarding the origins, traits, and developments of minds and their teleological functions.

Conclusion

I made a case in this chapter for teleology as an *emergent* rather than as a *primordial* factor in the universe, and did so by detailed engagement with aspects of the stimulating thought of Mikael Leidenhag. I developed analyses and responses to five principal classes of argument I interpret him to offer in defense of panpsychism, that is, the thesis that mind is an original, underived, continuously active presence throughout every stage of the history of the earth and in the whole of nature. The first argument is that mind could not have originated from matter because it is radically different from matter. The second argument is that telic norms or values cannot originate from original mere facts. The third is that a dual metaphysical basis is required for a proper understanding of mind-body interactions of all kinds, namely, an irreducible, underived mind in its constant relations with physical phenomena.

The fourth argument is that the primordial character and presence of mind are already implicit in the thesis and thought of emergentism, showing that mind itself does not emerge. And the fifth argument is Leidenhag's considered response to the charge that panpsychism is an arbitrary, merely penciled-in, unconvincing "solution" to the problem of understanding the presence of mind in nature.

I presented responses of my own to each of these five arguments in exposition of my view that mind has evolved from matter-energy interacting with the immense creative power of time over the history of our present universe, and thus that mind is an emergent phenomenon, not a primordial one. I was careful to note that I do not consider panpsychism to be a covert begging of the question but as a challenging species of argument purporting to account for the mental and teleological aspects of the present world. I did venture to suggest that belief in God might be a tacit influence in Leidenhag's spirited defense of panpsychism.

And I noted in this connection that religious naturalism is not necessarily a naturalizing of *God*, as the main title of Leidenhag's book indicates, but a naturalizing of *religion*. Religion and belief in God are not synonymous, despite the persistent tendency throughout the Western world even today to think that this is so. The main title of eloquent religious naturalist Chet Raymo's 2008 book joyfully proclaims, *When God Is Gone, Everything Is Holy*. This conviction is the fundamental theme of my own brand of religious naturalism. I am continuously enthralled—as is Raymo—with the countless sacred wonders of nature itself rather than with some sort of God commonly presumed to be their primordial source and sustainer.

Chapter Six

Organization as the Key to Mind

> To assume from the superiority of Galilean principles in the sciences
> of inanimate nature that they *must* provide the model for the sciences
> of animate behaviour is to make a speculative leap, not to enunciate
> a necessary conclusion.

> —Charles Taylor (1964: 25)

The whole is not simply the sum or aggregation of its parts. And analyses
suitable for investigation of the traits of its parts are not necessarily suitable for analyses of the traits and functions of the whole made up of those
parts. This fact reminds us, as Charles Taylor notes, that physics by itself,
as one kind of investigation into the traits and potencies of matter-energy
at a very basic level, is not necessarily able to investigate and explain all of
the traits and potencies of even the relatively less complex living bodies, to
say nothing of the higher levels of life on earth, and certainly not to offer
a sufficient explanation of the existence of conscious living bodies. Physics
is part of the story of evolution but by no means the only significant part.

The ascending orders of complexity and organization as we take into
account the history of biological, human, and cultural types of evolution
require an emergentist explanation of mind and of its teleological character
and capabilities. Reduction to the level of physics or to what Taylor calls
the "physical thing language" (89) assumed to be necessary in behavioristic
psychology assigns a competence to the findings and investigative techniques
of physics, not only of the Galilean or Newtonian type but also of the most
recent, revolutionary, twentieth-century type, to provide a sufficient account
for all mental and teleological phenomena.

Such approaches tend to assume that matter-energy is something static and unchanging through all time and not the dynamic, creative reality its evolutionary history clearly shows it to be. They focus only on a part of its immense historical development and not the whole of it up to the present time. In doing so, they fail to take sufficiently into account the continuing evolution of material systems and the effects of these new systems on their subsystems and on the constituents of those subsystems. Such developments make possible elaborate feedback relationships of the material systems and their parts. Physics itself is of course complex enough, but this complexity is greatly augmented when we get to the levels of life and mind. The character and capacities of matter itself are enormously altered and expanded by the transformative effects of the evolutionary process.

Appropriate understanding of the growing potentialities and competencies of matter is not restricted to the discipline of physics or to the behaviorist or operationalist methods of investigation often associated with and modeled on physics—and thought for that reason to be entirely appropriate for the study of all kinds of mental phenomena by virtue of their being commendably "scientific." At least to the extent of strongly disagreeing with such an assumption about the competence of physics and the reducibility of mental and teleological phenomena to an approach that is as close as possible to the tactics and findings of the field of physics, I have to agree with the proponents of panpsychism.

I shall return later in this chapter to Taylor's critical analysis of behaviorist psychology. It has fundamental bearing on the overall project of this book, as we shall see. But in the meantime, I want to develop some important observations of my own that relate to explanation and understanding of mental and teleological phenomena.

Chemistry makes necessary use of physics but is not the same thing as physics. Biology incorporates aspects of physics and chemistry but is not reducible to either or both of them. Psychology is closely related to physics, chemistry, and biology but is not identical with any of them or with the three of them taken together. The evolution of human beings presupposes the earlier evolution of life and then of conscious kinds of life but is not simply reducible to these earlier phases of biological evolution. Finally, linguistic, cultural, rational, volitional, and normative evolution among human beings brings about in its later stages characteristics and capabilities that were not present in its earlier ones. As I argued in the preceding chapter, evolutionary transformations and emergences over exceedingly long spans of time are required for a satisfactory explanation of all such later factors.

These factors cannot be reduced to their earlier phases of development because this development takes large expanses of time, and these expanses introduce new real possibilities and new actualizations of these real possibilities. The flow of time by its very nature involves fundamental innovations or introductions of newness, not mere repetitions of oldness. Were this not the case, there would be no such thing as the flow of time itself or as the commonly observed and constantly experienced distinctions of present and future moments, phases, and developments from past ones.

The emergence of new kinds of organization or system introduces complexities and functions of such systems as a whole that their parts alone did not possess and could not have exhibited apart from the relationships and interdependencies of the system. We can readily observe this fact when we consider the case of an animal body's wholistic functions in contrast with its parts regarded separately or in isolation from the body's overall organization or system. Liver, heart, brain, stomach, pancreas, muscle systems, eyes, and the like are nothing more than chunks of meat when removed from the body or when considered independently of their functions within the system of the body.

This analysis also holds true when we think of the body independently from the ambient environment that supplies it with the necessary oxygen, water, food, shelter, and protection essential to its survival. Finally, there would be no such thing as mind and its teleological functions apart from such interconnected systematic relations and dependencies. To take mind out of such contexts is to make the existence of mind something merely ad hoc or tacked on, and thus unintelligible and inexplicable. Apart from the evolution of organizing, facilitating, activating, and interacting systems of many different kinds, there would be no such thing as mental or teleological phenomena anywhere on the face of the earth.

Panpsychism, in my view, tends strongly and unconvincingly to be oblivious to such facts. Material or bodily organization is the key to mind and, as such, shows mind to be an emergent and not a primordial factor in the history of the earth's countless changes and developments over time. New, more complex biological systems continually emerge, and with them, new capabilities made possible by these systems, including increasingly more noticeable mental and teleological capabilities.

If this notion seems difficult to grasp, consider a simple example of how the organization of parts can impart a nature to the parts they could not have independently of their organization into some sort of whole. The example I have in mind is that of a deck of cards. Each card's character is dictated by its role in the game of cards. Apart from the structure provided by the rules of the game, the separate cards are nothing more than pieces of cardboard. They could be used separately as bookmarks, perhaps, but they are no longer essential parts of a game that confers on them their particular roles and values within the game. In similar fashion, were there no organic bodies, there would be no minds. Minds are made possible by highly organized and functioning bodies. They do not precede the evolution of such bodies, contrary to the panpsychist claim. These highly organized and systematically functioning bodies are produced by evolution, meaning that the minds they make possible are emergent rather than primordial.

If we grant all of these observations about the roles of parts within systems of organization, and the resulting traits, capacities, and functions of the parts made possible by these systems, we still leave hanging the crucial question of how organic wholes can impart to their parts such capabilities as those of life and mind. Addressing this problem, and especially as it relates to mind and its teleological character, is the task of this chapter. I am not competent to address it with the scientific detail it also requires, of course, but I do want to examine it from the standpoint of philosophy, that is, in the more general analytic and conceptual manner suitable to this discipline. I do so not in order to understand *intended purposes* served by evolutionary innovations, because I do not think of evolution itself as a purposeful enterprise.

But biological evolution has been a mutually adaptive enterprise, first by means of *living* beings capable of taking advantage of and affecting aspects of their natural environments, and then by increasingly *conscious* beings able to do so with conscious intentionality and foresight. Once brought into being, all life forms strive by their autopoietic natures to remain in being, and they affect one another's emerging species in their relations to one another, creating ecosystems within which all of them depend in order to flourish and survive. The emerging structures of these ecosystems affect and are affected by the emerging structures of new life forms within the ecosystems.

The ecosystems as well as their individual members can be threatened or improved by the emergence of new life forms, so their relative stabilities are always subject to ongoing changes. Ecosystems support life and are supported by the roles and actions of the life forms they contain. But they are also subject to ongoing transformation by those same life forms. Both parts and wholes in this case are dynamic rather than static in their character, each affected and being affected by the other.

Why does biological evolution continue to occur? There is no satisfactory overall answer to this kind of question. We should better ask *how* or by what processes does it continue to occur throughout the history of the earth. The proper question is descriptive instead of prescriptive. The adaptive ends served by evolution are outcomes of evolutionary processes, not preconditions for their occurrence. Evolution produces purposes rather than being created by some sort of all-encompassing cosmic purpose or end. Life precedes purpose, and nonconscious forms of life precede conscious ones. Keeping all of these very general points in mind, we can now proceed to examine some of the more particular factors involved.

With an eye to the philosopher Justus Buchler's magnificent book *Metaphysics of Natural Complexes*, another philosopher named Lawrence Cahoone has also written a splendid book on *metaphysics*, that is, a broadly conceived theoretical interpretation of the nature of reality. Buchler views reality as made up of "orders" of various kinds, each of which is a system, however large or small, that has intricate connections with other systems but not with all other systems. Since no system includes or encompasses all other systems, reality is pluralistic rather than monistic in character. Even the present universe can be more aptly termed a multiverse. Thus there is no such thing as an all-inclusive order of the world as a whole. The world is a plethora of orders of many kinds but not an order that contains all other orders.

I like this way of understanding reality because, among other things, it does justice to time. What do I mean about that statement? I mean that time is forever incomplete, always becoming, and in that way transcending and transforming, existing realities of the past. Time keeps my version of metaphysics from being monistic. It allows for a kind of emergent pluralism of new orders of being and becoming. Buchler's ordinal metaphysics also entails pluralism, because no existing order, however complex, inclusive, and comprehensive it may be, is capable of containing everything. And finally, since everything that exists is an order, complex, or system, there are no simples. Nothing exists that is not itself a system with varying degrees of complexity that acquires essential aspects of its character from the patterns of relationship in which it is set.

This claim gets back to the idea I discussed earlier, namely, that parts gain their significance within wholes and do not either exist or have their meanings independently of wholes, however small or large those wholes may be. What is true for all smaller parts is also true of larger ones and of the respective wholes in which each is embedded. For Buchler, moreover, there is no such thing as an all-inclusive, all-encompassing whole. These ideas of Buchler's are closely related to the title of the present chapter in that organization is the key to mind, as we shall see.

Getting back to Cahoone, he provides us with a book appropriately entitled in a Buchlerian manner, *The Orders of Nature*. He has a helpful diagram of what he regards as the five fundamental or most basic orders of nature (91). These orders are emergent ones, the second evolving from the first, the third from the second, and so on. In the remainder of this chapter I want us to think about each of these orders or ordinal stages of evolution, so that we can see how mind and all of its capabilities belong to the third through the fifth of Cahoone's orders and not to the two orders preceding them. He relegates mind to his fourth order and also, because of its embodiments and expressions in the order of culture, to his fifth level. To understand this argument is to see why panpsychism is false and not required to explain the presence of mind on the earth today.

I will adopt Cahoone's account of the major stages of cosmic evolution, and thus of reality as we experience it today, by altering it at some points and fitting it into my own account of evolution sketched in the preceding two chapters. His five basic orders of nature are the physical, the material, the biological, the mental, and the cultural. I replace the "physical" with "matter-energy," the "material" with "ordinary matter," and his two levels of "the biological" and "the mental" with "the biological." I add the category of "the conscious" to Cahoone's levels and do not include "the cultural" as a separate stage in my list of levels because I view it as already included in "the conscious," at least as regards increasingly conscious species of biological organisms. All of this may presently sound complicated and vague, but I will simplify and explain it as my discussion in this chapter proceeds. Each of the four levels of my own view of the basic stages of evolutionary change and development will comprise a separate section of description and analysis in what follows.

Matter-Energy and Ordinary Matter

The basement level of evolution or emergence is matter-energy. It is, as I have frequently asserted, primordial rather than derivative. And it is so along with the only other primordial factor in my metaphysical outlook, namely, time. The protean character of matter-energy makes it amenable to fundamental and far-reaching changes over large stretches of time. Matter-energy in its earliest stage was contained in extremely compressed form in the Big Bang origin of the present universe. That form itself, in my view, came into being under the influence of and by use and inclusion of critical ingredients of a previous universe that, like all of its previous ones extending successively into a hoary past without beginning, consisted basically of kinds and aspects of matter-energy.

Successive universes come into being and pass away with the passage of time. None of them exists forever or stays forever the same. Our own universe had a beginning and will at some future time have an ending. Creation and destruction go necessarily together even in the case of universes. What has come into being even in the case of a particular universe-pluriverse such as our own will someday cease to be. There is no absolute beginning or absolute ending of time, but there are absolute beginnings and endings of all things that come into existence and pass out of existence throughout time.

All that lies in the future of a universe at the time of its origin cannot be foreseen at that time. Its potentialities, like its actualities, emerge rather than being contained already at the point of the universe's origin. But all of these future potentialities, no matter how radical they may turn out to be, are made ultimately available to it because of the most fundamental potentiality that protean matter-energy provides. Matter-energy is the elemental continuity that underlies all of any universe's eventual and most strikingly novel transformations and changes. To be is to be material, and to become in the sense of becoming any kind of spatiotemporal existing thing—mental or otherwise—is to become a material thing. In other words, real existence, in contrast with something only imaginary or merely imagined to exist, is inseparable from material existence. This is an essential part of what I hold to be a credible story of evolution on earth.

My conception of the *first* stage of evolution as "matter-energy" is similar to Cahoone's conception of "The Physical" as the *first* and most comprehensive order of nature. It includes what he refers to as "Big Bang / Quantum Gravity, Quantum Fields / Space-Time / Radiation Era, Atoms / Matter Era, Stars / Galaxies, and Clusters of Galaxies / Black Holes." I would add to this list Dark Energy and Dark Matter. For Cahoone, what he calls "The Material" comes to the fore as the *second* stage of evolution only with the emergence of the "Heavy Elements," "Local Solar Systems / Sun," and "Solid State Matter / Earth; Minerals-Water-Air." Since systems of stars constitute galaxies and clusters of galaxies, and since the explosions of stars produce the heavy elements, his diagram has them overlap with or lie on the border with "The Material."

These *two* stages constitute collectively for me the first stage of evolution, namely, that of matter-energy as the earliest stage of activation of the Big Bang origin of the present universe. In my view this first stage includes the precursors of what I call "ordinary matter" as that becomes actual with the development of atoms, molecules, and more macrolevel or nonmicroscopic phenomena. Ordinary matter for me is a product of evolution from these precursors and calls attention to them as such. My point is similar to Cahoone's in that I emphasize ordinary matter as the evolutionary outcome of its subatomic and other precursors, meaning that it is evolution all the way down: from the Big Bang to free electrons, protons, forces, fields, and other initial nonatomic forms, to so-called ordinary matter as we encounter it in its atomic, molecular, and increasingly complex and more systemic, complex, tangible, everyday forms.

The Biological and Mental

I note again that there is no mention of *mind*, either in my conception of an evolved ordinary matter or in the stages prior to mind detailed in Cahoone's analysis. For him, mind emerges with what he calls "The Mental" or the fourth stage of evolution, and he associates it with "Vertebrates/Mammals." He then specifies a fifth stage he calls "The Cultural." For me, following the lead of Evan Thompson, mind is already a part of what Cahoone labels as his third evolutionary level, "The Biological," because this level incorporates for me in every aspect of its evolutionary development—from the most primitive to the most sophisticated forms of biological life—the mental traits of autopoiesis, sentience, and purposiveness.

But there is a significant difference between mind in these three rudimentary senses and *conscious* mind. So I list conscious mind as a different stage from the biological stage, as that is more generally and inclusively considered. Many living beings are conscious, but most of them presumably are not. Hence, I believe it is important that we take into account both the continuity of conscious mind with unconscious mind but that we also give appropriate attention to the critically important distinction between the two.

Because culture and consciousness have grown together and become increasingly salient together, I include the emergence and development of culture in this last stage of conscious mind. While my analysis and Cahoone's differ in important respects and are made evident in our different organizations of the history of evolution, both of the present universe and most specifically on earth, our basic evolutionary approaches to the nature, origin, and explanation of mental and teleological phenomena are notably similar. I proceed next, then, to consideration of the last phase in my analysis of the evolution of all such phenomena.

The Conscious and the Cultural

How plausible is it for me to believe, in contrast with Leidenhag, Nagel, Whitehead, and other reputable thinkers, that matter-energy, in concert with time, can produce and sustain both life and mind, with their teleological abilities—and that no kind of primordial mind is necessary for explaining this process? My response to this question lies at the heart of my objection to panpsychism, the objection being that it is not needed as an explanatory principle supplemental to an evolutionary principle in order to account for psychic phenomena. An evolutionary account rooted in a metaphysics in which matter-energy and time are the only necessary primordial principles can, in my view, provide a satisfactory account for the existence of mind, purpose, and value on earth. But is this claim really true? In the present section, we shall inquire more deeply into this all-important question.

But before doing so, I want to note a basic difference of my metaphysics from that of Buchler. In my view, everything that exists is some kind of temporally evolved and evolving matter-energy. There is an emergent pluralism, but the pluralism of levels or orders of existence is everywhere and everywhen a pluralism of types of matter-energy that are all outcomes of temporal processes. Buchler's pluralism is different. His pluralism is different from mine in at least one crucial respect. He does not endorse what I call "radical" materialism and defend in the last chapter of my 2013 book *The Philosophy of William James*. This same radical empiricism informs my discussions in this chapter and elsewhere in this book. It is radical largely because of its emphasis on the enormous potencies of matter that become actualities by means of evolution. The watchword of radical materialism is that matter *is* all that matter *does* or *undergoes* through time in the present universe. It is not something static and unchanging.

Radical materialism is a pluralism of material entities with different kinds of emergent functions or properties. As such, it is fundamentally different from the Newtonian type of materialism. Not only are the functions or properties different in important respects, but the matter they characterize changes in its forms, capacities, and operations with the emergence of new functions or properties. But it is still the fecund, protean matter-energy that pervades and underlies everything real. *It too emerges*, along with the new actualities that are brought into existence as it evolves.

But as it emerges or evolves, it continues throughout to be matter-energy in some shape or form, starting with its becoming what I call ordinary matter. Buchler's ordinal metaphysics is a pluralism of *orders* of any given type. Mine is a pluralism of orders of *material existence* of any given type. In other words, all of my orders emphasize the continuity of materiality throughout, while Buchler's emphasis is on the differences of each of the orders, continuously characterizable as orders, from one another. For me, mind and teleology are emergent forms of material existence. For further discussion and defense of this and other differences between Buchler's and my metaphysical outlooks, see my 2016 article (225–27).

Buchler's orders can and certainly do intersect with, interact with, and depend on one another, but their continuities are ones of their respective common characters as distinct *orders* of reality rather than of a pervasive, always underlying metaphysical *materiality*. The important difference I have sketched here also applies to Cahoone's metaphysics, because it too is a pluralism of distinct general orders of reality similar to Buchler's view, and not so much of different kinds of materiality. How adequately to account for both continuity and difference in a metaphysical manner is a fundamental issue underlying the difference.

I emphasize the continuity of matter-energy because I think this emphasis does more justice to the continuity implicit in the idea of evolutionary emergence of all the phenomena of nature. But I strongly resist, as do Buchler and Cahoone, the notion that all of reality is *reducible* to matter-energy, as though it were some sort of unchanging, forever the same kind of thing. Emergence is the evolution of genuinely new orders of material reality and of features and potencies of these new orders that cannot be reduced to earlier stages of the evolutionary process. The focus of my emergentist metaphysics is on what the future brings about from the past, while still acknowledging what the past has made possible in this way. In other words, it is primarily forward looking, not past looking. What is future *depends upon but is not reducible to* what is past. The ongoingness of time introduces fundamental, irreducible differences into the world. The flow of time and its outcomes are irreversible and thus irreducible.

The term *order* is etymologically akin to the word *organization*. Recognition of this fact brings me in the next section to discussion of how emergent systemic order can make mind of its countlessly different kinds possible. To put the question more precisely in keeping with the metaphysical outlook I am propounding, how does a certain ordering of *ordinary matter*, with its evolutionary dependence, in turn, on *matter-energy*, bring material life and mind in their various stages of emergence into existence? The short answer to the question is by means of the transformative, pervasive effects of organization or system on the components of an organization or system. But this succinct answer calls out for more analysis and explanation. So I turn next to examination of the relation of the emergence of a certain level or type of material organization to the emergence of mind (and its cultural aspects when present) as a function of these types of material embodiment.

Organization and Mind

Just as muscles in a living, highly evolved body cannot function properly without impulses from the neuronal system of the body, blood from the system of its heart, and oxygen from the system of its gills or lungs, so mind cannot function without essential connections and interdependencies within the system of the whole body and its interconnected subsystems of various kinds. I used a similar example earlier in this chapter, but it is also especially pertinent to the inquiry of this section. Organization is the key to the successful operations of parts of the body I am listing here, and it is equally crucial to the operations of mind in its most early autopoietic, sentient, and purposive functions, as well as to its more complex, highly evolved conscious and cultural ones. Complex systems constituting the environment of the living body are essential as well to its continual prospering and surviving.

The history of biological evolution is the history of the emergence of new kinds of organic bodies and of an increasingly complex systemic character of those bodies, each body being an intricate system of systems. Among the body's subsystems are systems capable of originating and sustaining mental phenomena of various kinds—all the way up to the phenomenological, firsthand character of our own experiences and activities of conscious minds as human beings. Just as my standing atop the high peak of a massive mountain in the Colorado Rockies is not reducible to my first standing at the bottom of the peak—otherwise, there would be no need for me to have expended the effort and energy of the climb—so my present mental capabilities, such as they are, are not reducible to those of a one-celled organism in the earliest stage of biological evolution.

Time, as I continue to emphasize, makes irreducibly real *new* realities, starting at the level of relatively simple ones to more and more complex ones. The more complex the latter evolved to become over time, the more complex their forms of material organization have become. And with these increasing levels of material complexity, more functions of mind are brought to development and expression. The complexity I speak of here is not just that of an increase of the numbers of *parts* in such organisms. It is a steady increase in development of their respective functioning *systems* of parts and wholes, and in the systematic interrelations of whole subsystems with one another to constitute a whole living organic system in its relations to other organisms and to its relevant ecological environment in general.

Such living systems are not called "organisms" haphazardly or by chance. They are organically (or systematically) functioning beings of a certain general type. Not only does time make a difference; it makes for systemic differences in the makeups of material beings, starting with the evolution of ordinary matter from its matter-energy precursor. And these systemic differences give rise, in their turn, to various types and levels of mind, including conscious minds. Biologists can supply us with much further detail by way of explaining how all of this is possible, but it requires no further discussion here. The basic idea of it is all I have intended to convey.

Still, perhaps another analogy will help to clarify how systems often make a crucial difference in how we interpret the function or meaning of the parts of something. This example is taken from the realm of human experience, but I hope that it will add clarity to the basic point I am endeavoring to make clear in this chapter. Suppose we are asked, "What is the difference between a democracy and an autocratic state?" And we answer, "In a democratic state the citizens have the responsibility and right to vote for the installment of their rulers into office. Officers that are voted in can be voted out later by the scheduled times for voting. Hence, would-be tyrannical or autocratic rulers are always susceptible to being defeated and put out of office in regular elections."

We might also appeal to a proper relation and functioning of legislative, executive, and judicial bodies in our answer to the question, but the answer I am focusing on here is sufficient to make the point I want to make. That point becomes clear as soon as we ask, "Who counts as a citizen? What counts as a vote? How are the scheduled times for voting determined? And, who or what confirms that the votes have been properly taken and recorded? And who or what insures that the results of the votes are put into practice in the ongoing life of the state?"

We can easily see that the correct or convincing answer to all of these questions depends on a certain kind of *system* of governance. It does not depend merely on the honesty and good nature of a loose collection of participants in a would-be state. A democratic state is more than a group of well-meaning individuals. It is an orderly system—or, more properly, a system of closely connected subsystems—carefully designed to facilitate the individuals' interactive, interdependent lives together and to insure their just and equitable governance. A certain kind of complex political system, with its essential subsystems, is the key factor in the concept of a democracy. What is true for such a body politic is also true, appropriate changes having been made, for a living bodily creature. Other such changes would also need to be made when it comes to characterizing conscious living bodies and ones capable of fashioning and living within cultures.

I want next to say a bit more about consciousness and then about its relation to culture in order to clarify their emergent roles in the history of life on earth. In doing so, I shall make further use of the thought of Charles Taylor by describing his trenchant criticism of behavioral or operational ways of interpreting and describing mental phenomena. These ways are, I shall argue, a kind of reductionism that should be included in my other criticisms of reductionism. They confine themselves in principle to what can be understood about such phenomena from the outside or in second-handed fashion, without taking sufficiently into account what these phenomena are like for conscious organisms at first hand. It is as if the latter have no significant scientific import in their own right.

By thinking in this way, behaviorism's proponents and practitioners tend to reduce psychology to the externalist conceptual level, attitudes, and procedures of physics. They thus ignore, at least implicitly, the transformative effects of evolution and the vast scientific significance of these developments. In doing so, they transport us back to the early scientific era's inadequate conception of matter, a concept that made a correspondingly inadequate mind-body dualism seem to be the only possible way to preserve the integrity and significance of mental phenomena. As Taylor points out, behaviorism tries to bridge what it sees as a yawning gap between mind and body by reducing and thus transforming manifestations of mind to material movements of the body that can be visually observed. But the gap itself is artificially and unnecessarily created by an inadequate and outmoded view of both matter and mind.

Taylor expresses his basic criticism of behaviorism or operationalism as the assumedly only possible way of studying mental phenomena in this way: "If the mental is something separate, and mental events are unobservable, then any explanation which uses psychological concepts, as explanation by purpose does, must involve unobservable entities. And insofar as the notion of 'purpose' involves that of direction by the agent, it must refer to an unobservable antecedent of action, the inner event of willing or purposing" (1964: 94). In thinking of mental events as unobservable and thus as inaccessible to scientific study, behaviorists tacitly endorse something reminiscent of the radical mind-body dualism of the early modern era in philosophy. We are left, as Taylor points out, with the notion that our only access to mental events is through various kinds of bodily *movements*. But he argues that we learn about the mental events of others, not solely or even mainly through their movements but for the most part through their directly perceived *actions*.

An action is a purposeful, agential phenomenon, not a matter of mere bodily movements. It is usually made immediately and obviously manifest as such, not as something that requires inference from something else entirely different from it like bodily movements. Purposeful action is not a mysterious, entirely "inner" phenomenon accessible to each individual person only at first hand. It is an outward phenomenon as well, routinely observable and accessible to others, including scientists. As such, there is no need to bring the study of mind down exclusively to the sorts of things physics and chemistry study.

The study of mind is a scientific field in its own right, with its own kind of subject matter. It should not be reduced to something nonmental, as though only that kind of approach can do justice to it or make it publicly intelligible. Behaviorism, in Taylor's judgment, is guilty of doing precisely this when it is viewed as the only possible or reliable mode of access to mental phenomena such as agential willing, purposing, and acting. Panpsychism gives tacit assent to such a view when it contends that matter must be supplemented with an entirely different factor or mode of existence called mind that must somehow be added or attached to it from another realm instead of being intrinsic to it as an outcome of biological evolution.

Taylor reinforces his case against behaviorism's reductionist program and on behalf of his view of the direct, everyday accessibility of mental phenomena—including consciously intended purposeful actions—that require no such reduction, with two telling examples (90). The examples exhibit no evident need to substitute for the mental something entirely physical and thus assumedly nonmental. The two examples concern, first, two humans interacting with one another and then a dog pleading for food from a human. The two humans are shaking hands. We conclude from this common practice that they are expressing their friendship and/or signaling their mutual respect for one another. We also conclude from this action that they *intend* to do so. The shaking of their hands is not just a physical *movement*. It is a purposeful *action*, commonly seen and accepted as such.

The second example depicts a dog desiring a piece of meat in Taylor's hand. It drools, snaps at the meat, and begs him for it. These reactions are not mere movements pertaining to the dog. They are reliable indications of the dog's *action* in response to the dog's *wanting* food. We do not learn about people's or dogs' actions "through their movements or through their autonomic reactions, or through the chemical processes which their bodies undergo," Taylor writes. Their actions are every bit as plainly and immediately observable "as movements of the hands of a clock" (90).

The confusion of actions with movements must be avoided, and this is a confusion behaviorism constantly encourages, in Taylor's view. Matter makes actions possible because actions are dependent on physical bodies for their origination and support. Minds are properties and functions of bodies. But actions are authentic, emergent mental phenomena that were not possible in the earliest evolutionary stages of ordinary nonliving matter. Once emerged, minds, intentions, and actions are not identical with their evolutionary precursors. They are genuinely new and readily observable realities in their own right. Behaviorism, as Taylor interprets it, fails to acknowledge or understand this fact. Mind is clearly dependent on matter but is not reducible to material movements. Nevertheless, mental phenomena are readily observable and intelligible and do not require inferences from such movements.

In the case of highly developed conscious minds, whether human or not, *cultures* of some sort or other are the frequent accomplishments and accompaniments of such minds. They insure that lessons learned from the experiences, discoveries, and mistakes of the past do not have to be *relearned in toto* by each new generation. They provide means of communication common to a species through its generations. They give to the parents of a species important means for educating their progeny and preparing them for their later independent lives. They are a network of critical resources to be drawn on by organisms as they face the challenge of surviving and thriving in what is often for them a precarious world.

As the complexities of new types of biological organisms increase with evolution, the complexities of their cultural developments—when present—

tend to follow suit and to increase through the ages. Thus mind and culture may develop together, each depending critically on the other. I discussed two striking examples of the essential role of culture among nonhuman animals in the third chapter of my book *The Multiplicity of Interpreted Worlds* by calling attention to and describing culture's functions in the lives of sperm whales and New Caledonian crows. I did so by making extensive use of two richly informative books by Carl Safina (2020) and Jennifer Ackerman (2017) on the central roles played by their cultures in the respective lives of members of these two species of natural beings.

The importance of aspects of culture and their integral connections with the development of minds is especially apparent in the lives of human beings. Humans are radically enculturated beings from their earliest days, both as a species and as individuals. Spoken language reaches so far back into the past of the human species that we are not able at present to trace out its earliest origins. Written language, in its turn, is a magnificent cultural achievement. Technology and toolmaking are critically important, constantly developing cultural achievements among humans. Record keeping, whether in memorized and frequently recited oral or carefully preserved written form, is not only a much-needed aid to memory; it is also a means of preserving the histories of human communities and making them available as resources, lessons, and guides for later generations. Religion, art, morality, and law are basic aspects of all human cultures, and each can attain high levels of complexity and attainment over many years. Culture is a kind of atmosphere that humans breathe from the day of their birth to the day of their death.

Among other things, human cultures are amazing feats of organization and structure, showing in their distinctive manners the role of organization as the key to mind, to recall the title of this chapter. Not only are developments of intricate networks of *material* organization crucial for the emergence of their individual minds as functions of their bodies in the case of humans—as with other organisms—but the emergence of intricately organized collective human *cultures* has contributed immeasurably to the cultivation and development of humans' mental capabilities.

Human language is a good example. It has become incredibly complex over the millennia of its development and been an essential aid to the development of human thought, awareness, and creativity. We cannot begin to fully understand the lives of humans today without taking extensively into account the enormous contributions of their cultural accomplishments to the whole of their lives and especially to the mental aspects of their lives, both individually and collectively. Once again, emergence is the critical factor in explaining the development and presence of mind in humans and at least to some extent in all other organisms. The theory of panpsychism or of the *primordial* character of mind, in contrast with the growing evolutionary emergence of types of mind as natural outcomes of the organizations of living bodies through time, is not required. Mind is a natural outcome of evolutionary processes, not a prior condition for their later developments.

Conclusion

In this chapter, as in those preceding it, I have placed strong emphasis on mind as an emergent phenomenon, not a primordial one. I have done so here by calling attention to the essential role of increasingly complex levels of interactive systems and subsystems for explaining the presence of mind and for the various kinds of agential, purposive actions mind makes possible in biological organisms, including our own human species.

Teleology, therefore, is a function of mind, and mind is a function of ordinary matter, which in its turn is a function of the matter-energy contained in the Big Bang, which initiated the earliest stages of development of the present universe that led to the emergence of ordinary matter. The evolutionary saga of ordinary matter has led to biological evolution, with its earliest stages of mind and eventually to increasingly complex types of conscious mind. The developments of conscious mind have been enhanced and augmented by the various types of culture developed among some conscious beings. So these four stages of evolutionary change and development have led, over enormous stretches of time, to our own mental, teleological, and cultural capabilities as human beings: (1) matter-energy, (2) ordinary matter, (3) living beings, and (4) conscious living beings—some of the latter with supporting cultures of different kinds. None of these stages is immaterial, and none has given rise to anything immaterial.

All of them are emergent products of matter-energy that have unfolded as outcomes of the creative (and destructive) power of time. The flow of time is itself a continuing combination of continuity and novelty, and both of these aspects, working with the protean character of matter, have made the present universe an emergent universe—a universe that has never stood still or ceased to bring about wondrous possibilities and actualities of change. Mentality and teleology are effects of these changes on earth and are in no sense prior to them or already contained within them at every stage of their emergence. If this statement is true, then it follows that panpsychism is false.

But how did ordinary matter produce life, mind, conscious mind, and the cultural creations of conscious mind? The key to these processes is organizations or systems of increasingly complex kinds. I made use of the thought of Justus Buchler and Lawrence Cahoone in arguing for this essential point. Both of them talk of orders of being and becoming, and of orders interacting with other orders, creating in the process new products of emergence. These, in their turn, exhibit increasing levels of complex, mutual interaction among their subsystems or suborders. Biological organisms are rightly called such because they are systems of order within order wherein their constituent orders gain new powers as the result of their interactions. A system or order of a particular kind functions differently within the context of higher level systems or orders than it would apart from such a context. We know this from the organizational factors essential to the functioning of machines, and we know it from observing the crucial structural inter-dependencies of living bodies. Everywhere around us we observe the fact that a part may be quite different in its capabilities and meanings when considered either within or outside of the context of a surrounding system.

I used a deck of cards and a political system by way of making this point, and it is of course perfectly clear when we take into consideration any living body of whatever level of relative simplicity or complexity. It clearly applies to both bacteria and human beings. So what is mind and where does it come from? The proper answer to this question, in my humble view, is that mind is a systematic phenomenon in its own right that is critically reliant on the enormously complex, intricately interactive system of subsystems of the organic body. This body is the emergent product of matter-energy being continuously affected and transformed by time. Time makes a difference, and it does so largely by its development of systematic interactions and dependencies of matter. The key to mind is organization, and organization is the key to all else that we experience here on earth.

Chapter Seven

Teleology and Two Kinds of Religious Faith

Despair is potentiate in proportion to consciousness of self; but the self is potentiated in the ratio of the measure proposed for the self, and infinitely potentiated when God is the measure. The more conception of God, the more self; the more self, the more conception of God. Only when the self as this definite individual is conscious of existing before God, only then is it the infinite self, and then this self sins before God.

—Søren Kierkegaard (1951: 129)

The nineteenth-century Danish poet, philosopher, and theologian Søren Kierkegaard stands in the stead of such great Christian thinkers of the past as Augustine of Hippo, Meister (Johannes) Eckhart, and Martin Luther in his interpretation of the Christian faith and, in particular in his book *The Sickness unto Death*, from which the epigraph to this chapter is excerpted.[1] I want in the first section of this chapter to acknowledge and discuss one important and prevalent kind of *panpsychism*, the kind that is intimately connected with *belief in God*. The version of theism I shall make use of in order to explicate this connection is Christian theism. Other versions of theism could also be brought into play, but this one is sufficient for illustrating the connection to which I want to call attention here.

Theism and Panpsychism

Augustine writes in the beginning paragraph of his *Confessions* as follows:

> Great art Thou, O Lord, and greatly to be praised; great is Thy power, and thy wisdom infinite. And Thee would man praise; man, but a particle of Thy creation; man, that bears about him his mortality, the witness of his sin, the witness that Thou resistest the proud: yet would man praise Thee; he, but a particle of Thy creation. Thou awakes us to delight in Thy praise; for Thou madest us for Thyself, and our heart is restless, until it repose in Thee. (1961: 11)

Eckhart contended in similar fashion that the proper worship and service of God takes place only when our will becomes firmly aligned with the will and purpose of God, for we have no authentic will or self apart from the will of God. God's will must become our will. In one of his sermons or talks, he states, "The will is perfect and right when it has no selfhood and when it has gone outside of itself, having been taken up and transformed into the will of God" (1994: 16). In another one, he implores, "We must train ourselves in self-abandonment until we retain nothing of our own. All turbulence and unrest comes from self-will, whether we realize it or not. We should establish ourselves, together with all that is ours and all that we might wish or desire in all things, in the best and most precious will of God through a pure ceasing-to-be of our will and desire" (1994: 42). The phrase "turbulence and unrest" in this statement reminds us of Kierkegaard's "sickness unto death." The dreadfully sick, mortally wounded self is the self that is detached from God and that tries futilely to live a meaningful life apart from God. There is no self-realization without God-realization. To be at one with God is the only way to be truly human.

Luther insisted that salvation is possible only by faith in the atoning work of Christ on the cross, not by means of anything we humans do, no matter how ardently and persistently such human deeds may be performed. So great is the sinful state of our separation from God that only God can restore us to right relation with God. We are helpless otherwise. Our only recourse is to place our faith in God and in God's work within us, not in anything solely or separately of our doing. Faith in God is nothing other than reposing complete trust in the promises of God on which all of our hope for salvation and true self-fulfillment rest. Good works flow from such trust or faith, but "we must not think," he warns, "that a man is justified before God by them" (1947: 269).

Spontaneous love and respect for God's trustworthiness is the font of all good works and of realization of one's nature as a creature of God, for this and this alone enables us to live a truly human and thus truly God-centered life—the life of such a creature as God means for us to be. For Luther, this life of faith as the font of all that is holy and good in us, and in our relation to our creator, is the only cure for what Kierkegaard calls the dread mortal sickness of a self that is alienated from God.

In his famous "Treatise on Christian Liberty," Luther insists that absence of faith is a fatal rejection of God because it refuses to trust in everything God gives to us, has given up for us, and makes possible for us. Without trust, there can be no genuine love, and without genuine love for God, there can be no salvation. Salvation for Luther is a matter first and foremost of the heart's relation to God. Its *fruit*, not its prior *condition*, is obedience to God and the good works that reflect such obedience. He writes, "Since by faith the soul is cleansed and made a lover of God, it desires that all things, and especially its own body, shall be as pure as itself, so that all things may join with it in loving and praising God" (1943: 269).

Kierkegaard writes similarly, not only in the epigraph quoted earlier but also when he speaks a bit further along in the same work of the infinitely deep sense in which "a human self is morally under obligation to God with respect to every secret wish and thought, with respect to quickness in comprehending and readiness to follow every hint of God as to what His will is for this self" (131). And he emphatically agrees with Luther that the opposite of sin is not some collection of good works, however fervently and conscientiously pursued or attained, but consists solely in faith in the salvific power of God's becoming a man in Jesus Christ and offering us his arduous ministry and his agonizing death on the cross as a sacrifice for our sins. The opposite of sin is therefore faith (132), not just an accumulation of good works that might falsely be thought to offset sin as a collection of bad works. Thus both sin and faith are *states of being*, that is, either the state of tragic separation from God or the state of blissful trust in God's redemptive promise of salvation through the work of Christ.

Sin for Kierkegaard is a state of being "before God," and its only true remedy is faith in God, "for every sin is before God, or rather it is this which properly makes human guilt to be sin" (128–29). For each of these writers, sin is separation from God through lack of trust in God's promises, and salvation or true goodness is God's gift to us, not simply our accomplishment. Our works are basically worthless when performed without an alignment of our mind and spirit with the will and purpose of God. Faith is trust in God's willingness to do on our behalf what we have no capacity to do apart from God or on our own.

Sin for Kierkegaard, as for Augustine, Eckhart, and Luther, is the state of being estranged from God as humanity's and the whole of nature's creator and sustainer. And this estranged state, properly analyzed and understood, is nothing other than the state of all-consuming *despair*. It is none other than a tragic "sickness unto death," that is, a continuous self-destructive outlook and mood of relentless, deep-lying hopelessness. It is such because there is no truly free, contented, or joyful self—no realization of one's true humanity as the child of God—in alienation from God. Only the work of God, not our human works, can heal the agonizing, fatal wound of this alienation.

Kierkegaard is well aware that the Christian message is at bottom *literally* meaningless. It is such because it requires, at least as he regarded it, putting trust in a seeming contradiction and committing one's life to the contradiction. The contradiction is the idea of a *God-Man*, namely, the historical Jesus of the first century CE. But how could God be God and yet also become, and be at the same time, man? Kierkegaard's well-known response to this quandary is to say that we must take a leap to faith, trusting in the truth of the traditional Christian message without demanding that it be made credible or even intelligible on a purely human plane (1951: 192, 206). We must somehow yield our minds as well as the rest of our being wholly to God because only by this total yielding can we experience salvation of our souls and rescue from despair.

The centerpiece of all of human life for Augustine, Eckhart, Luther, and Kierkegaard is God. This is Christian monotheism at its heart. Its contrast with the kind of religious naturalism in which *nature*, not some conception of a personal, loving, saving *God*, is readily apparent. For religious naturalism, everything that exists is an aspect of nature. For Christian theism of the traditional sort, everything that exists does so only as the creation of God or as some aspect of divine creation—however distorted that aspect may be or have become through wanton, willful, destructive human agency, agency that runs counter to the will and purpose of God. Humans exist, to use Kierkegaard's telling phrase, "before God." There is no authentic human self apart from God. Loss of self is the inevitable result of loss of God. And this concomitant loss is the root and meaning of despair.

Similarly, all of *nature* is for Kierkegaard "before God," and there would be no such thing as nature or of any kind of natural being apart from God. Human sinfulness as well as human salvation takes place ultimately and regularly in relation to God. Take away God, and everything else is taken away, just as for the religious naturalist, take away nature, and everything is taken away. Theistic metaphysics and naturalistic metaphysics are in this fundamental respect opposed to one another. Despite this radical difference, however, many of the other purposes, meanings, and values of the two religious stances are similar. Ample room remains for ongoing dialogue between their proponents.

One thing that is irreducibly different, however, is their respective *teleologies*. This difference is what I want to focus on in this chapter. And I want to stress as strongly as possible its *existential*, and not merely its *conceptual*, implications. Unless we take seriously the full import of the former, we will fail to see how deeply rooted the difference is, and why it matters so much to the traditional Christian theist. In the theistic vision, all purpose, meaning, and value of any kind stem ultimately from God, and thus from the *mind* of God. And everything that exists springs from and is critically dependent on and made possible by the mind of God. *Mind is therefore primordial, not derivative, in its ultimate character and significance.*

For the religious naturalist, at least of the sort that I am envisioning in this book, everything stems ultimately from nature, and nature ultimately consists in all of its forms, orders, or kinds as types of matter-energy interacting with time. Mind is emergent from these two primordials of nature. It is not original but is derived from processes of nature, first in the form of emergent *living* beings and then in the form of *conscious* living beings such as ourselves and other conscious animals of different capabilities and kinds. We may currently lack explanation and understanding of all of the exact details of this emergent process as it unfolds over time. But we can be reasonably confident of the basic outlines of how it came to be. One consequence of this confidence is that we can revere *the sacredness of nature* and have our religious sensibilities center there rather than on some kind of personal God regarded as the creator and sustainer, not only of every past or presently existent thing but also of all that could ever possibly exist.

In the theistic vision, the only primordial, nonderivative reality is God. Both matter-energy and time are creations of a purely spiritual, timeless, or time-transcending God. God relates to matter-energy and time once God has created these two, and also to beings such as ourselves that have minds capable of intentional or purposive actions. But apart from God, no such factors, powers, or beings would exist or could do so, even from one moment of time to the next.

I like to compare this theistic view to a mobile that hangs from the ceiling and has various kinds of objects suspended in delicate balance from its arms. If we release the mobile from its attachment to the ceiling, the whole thing collapses into a featureless, meaningless heap. God is the "attachment" from which all else hangs. In the absence of God, for the committed theist, everything would be chaotic, meaningless, devoid of order. And that everything includes everything of value. The world and everything in it would be devoid of purpose and significance of any kind.

The popular English apologist for a Christian theistic view of the world C. S. Lewis comes at the connection between belief in God and the cosmic primordiality of mind when he describes his conviction, even before his conversion to Christianity, that epistemological *realism* is true and *idealism* is false. "Rock-bottom realism," as he characterized it then, and to which he found himself at the time strongly committed, meant that "abstract thought (if obedient to logical rules) gave indisputable truth, that our moral judgment was 'valid,' and our aesthetic experience not merely pleasing but 'valuable.'" The only convincing alternative to taking what he calls a wholly inadequate behaviorist, idealist, or subjectivist view of such matters, Lewis came to believe, was to admit to himself "that mind was no late-come epiphenomenon, that the whole universe was, in the last resort, mental; that our logic was participation in a cosmic logos" (1955: 208–09).

He finally realized that this conviction was nothing other, at least for his way of thinking, than theism or belief in God. In other words, he became what I have been calling throughout this book a kind of *panpsychist*, a panpsychist whose outlook is deeply informed by commitment to God as the creator of the universe and everything in it—and therefore as the *Divine Mind* that pervades, underlies, and accounts for everything in the universe. Mind is thus the primordial source of all that exists and is not derivative from anything more fundamental than itself.

It is ironic that Lewis's conclusion is so similar, at least in its logic, to Jean-Paul Sartre's assumption that a universe without God is by virtue of that conclusion devoid of any kind of objective purpose or meaning. For Lewis, this conclusion was a mandate to believe in the existence of God, put faith in God, and abide by God's guidance and light. For Sartre, it meant that there is no other recourse for us humans than having arbitrarily and absurdly to *invent* whatever life-governing meanings and values we could come up with, and then *choose* to live by them. In offering the analysis of this chapter so far, I do not intend to defend theism. I intend only to explicate some of its logic, as understood and claimed by many of its adherents, and to show how that logic gives supposed support to panpsychism or at least to the primacy of mind and cosmic purpose (or telos) in relation to everything else.

Behind the logic, much more often than not, lies the profound religious hope and yearning for existential, and not just conceptual, meaning.

We need to keep this fact firmly in mind even as we seek to understand religious naturalism as an alternative religious perspective, stance, and commitment. More is at stake in both perspectives than philosophical (or scientific) analysis, comparison, argument, and comprehension, important as such approaches are. What is ultimately at stake is a vision of the world, of our human selves as parts of the world, and a whole way of life.

In order to understand this to be the case for religious naturalism, and not just for theistic ways of viewing and experiencing the world—acknowledging in this manner the profound existential import, assurance, and demand of each of these religious perspectives—I turn next to religious naturalism. By doing so, I can show how religious naturalism's focus on nature as the central concern of religious faith relates to theism's focus on God, and how it also relates to the themes of teleology and panpsychism that are basic to this book. There are of course many other kinds of theism than the version of Christian theism I have described here and attributed to the four Christian thinkers discussed. But these four provide useful examples of theism's perspective on teleology as primordial rather than emergent, and of its principal focus on God rather than on nature. This perspective is profoundly existential, and not merely a matter of doctrine or belief. On it hangs the hope of salvation and relief from despair.

Religious Naturalism and Panpsychism

In order to explicate some of the central convictions that give conceptual expression to the faith stance of religious naturalism, at least as I view it, I will contrast these convictions with ones relating to the same or similar topics in theism. The first and most obvious contrast is over what is metaphysically ultimate. For the naturalist, this is *nature*, while for the theist, it is *God*. For the naturalist, everything that exists originates from nature, while for the theist, everything in nature, including nature itself, is produced by the creative intentions and actions of God. And because God is regarded as a supremely purposive, spiritual, mental person, teleology—like everything else—has its primordial source in God. For the naturalist, however, teleology emerges from nature rather than being prior to nature.

Such priority includes priority over both time and matter-energy in theism, while in the religious naturalism I am endorsing and describing, time and matter-energy are metaphysically prior to everything else, and these two bring mind, with its intentional goals and behavior, into being. In theism, nature as a whole is a purposeful creation of God, and all of the important purposes of human life are conferred on humans by God. In religious naturalism, purpose on earth first emerges with the evolution of life, and it first becomes conscious and intentional in the different conscious forms of life. The overarching purpose of human life for theism is faithful, trusting alignment with and loving obedience to the will of God. In religious naturalism it is reverence for the pervasive sacredness of nature and continuing cultivation of thoughts, dispositions, actions, and commitments that can give expression to this reverence throughout human life.

Traditional theists have strongly tended to view the natural world as a point of departure toward an afterlife of radical bliss and fulfillment in a realm far removed from their earthly mode of existence, a realm in which unbroken communion with God is finally attained. Its fundamental orientation and expectation are thus away from the earth and toward heaven, away from all tragedy, suffering, sorrow, and disappointment of existence in the bodily form of earthly life. The constraints of time will also be transformed and overcome in this new mode of life. It will be either timeless or everlasting, thus sharing in the timelessness or everlastingness of God, that is, either being outside of time altogether or enduring forever without a temporal end in the future.

In contrast, religious naturalism is grateful for the temporally bounded extent of the lives of human beings on earth, and it cultivates feelings of commonality and close communion with the other creatures of earth that come into being and pass out of being in time. As with them, religious naturalism expects humans to be born, live, and inevitably to die. Finitude and fallibility apply to all creatures of earth, including humans and their particular projects and aims. The tragedies and sorrows of natural life, as well as its beginnings and endings, are their lot just as they are the lot of all other natural beings. But there are achievements, joys, and fulfillments possible for humans within the temporal spans of this life as well.

For religious naturalism, there is no escape from the ambiguities of nature or from the ambiguities that pertain to them as they do to all other natural beings. These ambiguities are made necessary by the intersecting, interdependent, and often conflicting orders that make all else in the vastness of nature possible. Without ongoing deaths, for example, there could be no such thing as a continuation of the innumerable forms of life on the finite earth, human and nonhuman. Predation is part of the food chain, for another. Precariousness and finitude go naturally together, as still another example. For the religious naturalist, all of this is gift and challenge enough, just as it must be enough for all of the life forms of earth. It cannot be otherwise because there is no alternative. Life is a perilous adventure, but it also makes available deeply meaningful satisfactions and rewards, all of them gifts of nature. Among the gifts of nature is emergent life itself, including the lives of human beings, with their capacities of consciousness, reason, purposiveness, and hope.

There is a kind of "great chain of being"[2] integral to traditional theism that is not present in religious naturalism. For the former, humans stand at the apex of nature and have a status "little less than God" (Psalm 8: 5, see also Hebrews 2: 7, RSV), with dominion over all of the creatures of the earth. Humans are only partly physical in their true character. They—unlike all other beings of the earth—have a spiritual aspect that is akin to the spiritual character of God and of the heavenly host. It shows humans as having a "transcendence over natural processes," in the words of twentieth-century Christian theologian Reinhold Niebuhr (1949: 270). Thus for theism, humans are not fundamentally citizens of nature or of this earth, but of another form of existence beyond the world. Their true destiny and communion lie not with the creatures of nature but with other human beings and ultimately with God, and with all those who find their final salvation and repose in heaven as a nonphysical, purely *spiritual* realm.

For religion of nature, in contrast, the true home of humans is on earth, and their true communion is with one another and with all of the other fellow creatures of nature. What theists owe to God religious naturalists owe to nature. What is most sacred to theists is God; for religious naturalists, it is nature. Theists exist "before God." Religious naturalists exist "before nature." To be without God, according to religious naturalism, is not to be consigned to despair. It is to live as a reverent, respectful, grateful creature of nature—at home here on earth with all the other creatures of earth. Salvation does not lie beyond the grave. It lies in the here and now and most fundamentally in feeling at home on earth as a natural being with the bountiful natural gifts of a human being.

The distribution and extent of these gifts varies from person to person, and there is more, and in some cases much more, tragedy and suffering in the lives of some humans than in the lives of others. This fact has to be acknowledged by theism as well. There is expected respite from this variable human condition in the promise of heaven for at least some versions of theism. There is no such promise in religious naturalism. But for the latter, there is also no need to explain or question why God allows such tragic inequities, and why God did not create humans as angels in heaven in the first place.

The ambiguities of nature stubbornly and tragically exist in both perspectives. Theists can claim strength and courage from a loving God to persevere in the face of these ambiguities. Religious naturalists claim these qualities from the indwelt strength given to them as resourceful natural beings, from the help of other caring humans, and from the deeply inspiring majesty, sublimity, and wonder of every aspect of the natural order. No primordial telos or universe with some kind of overarching, all-encompassing purpose for its being is required for the naturalist. An emergentist rather than a primordial teleology is sufficient and sustaining in its own right. The tragedy and suffering remain, and they are acknowledged to be doled out in unequal measures to the creatures of nature in both the theistic and the naturalistic perspectives. In the theistic ones, they are the inexplicable allowances of God, at least when not viewed as outcomes of human sin. In the perspective of religious naturalism, they reflect the finitude of nature and the fact that in its vast system of natural orders, what gives sustenance and support to some at some times can inflict tragedy and hurt on others at other times. This realization does not mitigate the suffering and inequity, but it also does not make it the unfathomable mystery it can become when traced ultimately to the will and purpose of a loving God.

Three other basic differences characterize theism, on the one hand, and religious naturalism, on the other. I have already alluded to them in this chapter and elsewhere in this book, but now I want to discuss them in more detail. The first one pertains to the humanlike or anthropomorphic conception of God. The second is theism's reliance on an alleged authoritative revelation directly from God and its implications for the competency and scope of human reason. The third involves the attitude proponents of traditional theism typically have had toward other religious commitments and points of view. I shall first sketch these three traits of traditional theism. I shall then devote a separate section to further discussion of religious naturalism's vision of life devoted to the sacredness of nature instead of to some kind of personal God.

Traditional Theism's Personal God, Reliance on Divine Revelation, and Attitude toward Other Religions

The God of traditional theism or, more precisely, *monotheism*, attributes to God many of the attributes of human beings. God is a personal being with mind, will, and feelings closely akin to these traits of humans. God is a loving, guiding, judging, merciful, and even sorrowing being, showing in these ways capabilities similar to those of humans. God can be the responsive focus of praise, gratitude, confession of sins, entreaty, and prayer. God is the personal, conscious creator of the universe and of everything that is part of the universe. God deeply desires communion with God's human creatures, creatures made in God's own image.

It should be noted that the conception of God in traditional theism is very much like that of a human being, although raised to an extraordinarily high degree. This conception is nevertheless anthropomorphic to the core. God is not like a camel, giraffe, or horse. There are ample warnings in such theism to preserve the immense distance between God and humans, and this distance is said to be absolute, and not merely one of degree. But the close resemblance to humans in many respects remains, despite such frequent warnings. If humans are in the image of God, it is also true that God, to a significant and undeniable extent, is conceived in the image of humans.

The radical transcendence of God is combined, paradoxically, with an intimate, all-pervading immanence. God's concourse with God's human creatures is not surprising, given the extent to which they resemble God and are seen as the crown of God's creation of the world. And "the world" has for millennia been viewed as centered on the earth, and especially on the human beings of earth. Little attention is given even today among many traditional theists to the immensity of the universe as we now view it scientifically. This is to say nothing of the strong possibility of forms of life—many of them perhaps either similar to humans or far exceeding human characters and capabilities—in a universe of billions of galaxies, stars, and life-supporting planets that probably orbit at least some of those stars.

Moreover, traditional confessional theism is based to a large extent on purported special revelations of God's nature and of God's expectations for human life that are graciously bestowed on them by God. For Judaism, Christianity, and Islam, this revelation is contained, respectively, in the Hebrew Bible or Tanakh, the Christian New Testament, or the Holy Qur'an. Christians view the New Testament as the fulfillment of the teachings of the Hebrew Bible, while Muslims regard the Qur'an as the final culminating revelation of authoritative, anticipatory divine disclosures also contained in the Jewish and Christian scriptures.

Humans are encouraged to use their reasoning abilities for interpreting these sacred texts, but their reason is subordinate to divine revelation and is reliable only to the extent that it rests on the ultimate authority of the revelations of God's purpose and will contained in the texts and in proper interpretations of the truths and values set forth in the texts. Unaided human reason is not a dependable guide to leading an authentic religious life of worship and service to God. To aspire to know God's purpose and will for human life apart from God's gracious and loving definitive revelations is like trying to claw up an immense vertical pane of glass with bare hands and feet alone, with no kind of external aid. God must reach down before humans can learn how to reach up.

If the kind of God theism professes to believe in truly exists, traditional theism reasons, it would make no sense for God to leave humans without God's revelatory guidance and support. Traditional theism is therefore a *revelatory theism*, not one arrived at or attainable by unaided human reason, no matter how incisive and telling that reason might seem to be when relied on alone. Nature can be seen as giving witness to the glory of God, but only when guided by the appropriate kind of direct, unmediated, personal disclosure of God's purpose and will for human life.

God is immanent in the world, and the world testifies in innumerable ways to God's presence and care, but for traditional theism, only God's special revelations can provide the kind of explicit guidance and truth required for living an authentic religious life. Christians like Augustine, Eckhart, Luther, Kierkegaard, and Niebuhr take for granted the conviction that God has made Godself known, not only by God's creation of the world and by the innumerable manifestations of God's reality in the world, but also by God's definitive revelations to human beings in sacred texts and in dependable, lasting traditions that are believed to rest on those texts.

There is an obvious problem, however, in traditional theism's appeal to special revelations of God's nature and God's purpose and will for human-kind. The problem is that not all claimants to special revelations from God agree on what the special revelations are and where they are to be found. For Jews, they are proclaimed in the Jewish scriptures, for Christians, they reside in the Jewish scriptures as supplemented and fulfilled in the Christian ones, and for Muslims, their final and definitive character and meaning are contained in the Qur'an, seen as the necessary supplement to and culmina-tion of the Jewish and Christian scriptures. Jews, Christians, and Muslims, therefore, do not agree on what the finally authoritative special revelations of God consist of. Sacred texts and putative revelations of religious truth are characteristic of many other religious traditions, so the problem with appeals to them is that they are *many*, and they *do not all agree with one another*.

In fact, their disagreements are every bit as striking in numerous fun-damental ways as are their agreements. If one insists on the absolute truth of his or her own religious tradition, especially as claimed to be grounded in divine revelation, this one tradition becomes the necessary standard by which all other traditions, with their own claimed special revelations, are to be measured. And in this conviction lies the seed of a claimed right of domination and control by proponents of one religious tradition over all others.

This claimed right has lain behind much of the conflict, violence, persecution, and warfare that have defiled human history and continue to ravage it today. One thinks in this connection of the Muslim conquests, the Christian Crusades, the Thirty Years' War among Christians, the frequent pogroms against the Jews by so-called Christians, and conflicts among Sunni and Sufi Muslims that turn on different interpretations of the Qur'an. Also brought to mind are the terrorist programs of Isis and al-Qaeda that aspire to replicate in the current Middle East the seventh-century caliphate assumed to be grounded in the Qur'an, and the brazen conquests of other peoples and nations by avowedly Christian colonial powers. The conflict between Jews and Palestinians in the supposed Holy Land is another case in point, especially to the extent that the conflict turns on unyielding, uncompromising appeals to either the absolute authority of the Tanakh or that of the Qur'an.

What I want to emphasize here, as well as in the next section on religious naturalism, is that matters such as the ones indicated here, and those to be indicated in what follows, are matters of profound *existential* import and not merely ones of *intellectual* disagreement. They bear on the whole of life and guide basic practices and ways of living, not just ways of thinking and believing. In light of this fact, these matters of disagreement and difference cannot be easily dismissed or causally set aside but have to be regarded with appropriate seriousness and respectful convictional openness on all sides. Different religious convictions may and often do overlap in some ways or to some extent, and it is important to explore and recognize this fact. But non-overlapping convictions can have as fundamentally important significance for another person or group as the cherished different ones are likely to have for one's own self or group. As I now continue to discuss religious naturalism's outlook, a version of which I shall defend here and have done in other writings, I want us to keep this crucial fact firmly in mind.

Religious Naturalism's Vision of Life Devoted to the Sacredness of Nature

What is sacred deserves to be honored and revered, not disrespected and profaned. The whole of nature is sacred ground for the religious naturalist. This sacredness includes every aspect of nature, including its living and nonliving aspects, and it encompasses its frightening and destructive ambiguities as well as its serene and comforting wonders. As the philosopher Rudolf Otto described the sacred (or holy) in his famous book *The Idea of the Holy*, first published in German in 1917, it is marked by awesome, dreadful, overpowering majesty and might, as well as by fascinating and alluring promise of assurance and salvation (1958: 12–40). Above all else, the sacred has an aspect of confounding mystery. Otto summarized his conception of the holy in the memorable Latin phrase *mysterium tremendum et fascinans*.

Nature is sacred in these three senses—overwhelmingly powerful, endlessly fascinating, and unfathomably mysterious—for the religious naturalist. It is the ultimate source of all human life just as it is for all of the other forms of earthly life. Its countless wonders testify to its mystery, majesty, and greatness. Earth is home for the human spirit and the only such home. To be "saved" for religious naturalism is to contemplate and experience as many as possible of the implications of being at home here and only here, and of being such in empathetic, caring, considerate communion with the other creatures of earth. Religious naturalists rejoice in the privilege of being for a limited time conscious creatures of the earth, and they do not anticipate or yearn for an endless future life in some other realm. As theists strive for alignment with God, religious naturalists strive for the closest possible alignment of heart, spirit, and practice with nature.

But they are also well aware that the earth is not the universe, that there is much more on earth than human beings, including all of the millions of other forms on earth; that the orders of earth can sometimes hinder and hurt the lives of its finite creatures; and, most basically, that it is not all about human beings on earth or about any particular human being. One should not expect, therefore, to be exempt from the ambiguities of a multiply ordered finite universe. As Otto argues with respect to the very nature of the holy, there are comfort and peril, gifts and inequities, understanding and bafflement, joy and suffering, serenity and sorrow for humans as for all other creatures in the sacredness of the natural world.

Moreover, humans should not expect to live forever any more than they expect other creatures of the earth to do so. Their lives are bounded by birth and death, and within this limited span they are invited to do the most they can by living their lives to the fullest as creatures of nature who honor, cherish, and celebrate the sacredness of nature in the ways available to them as such creatures. These ways include, of course, honoring and respecting one another as human beings. Humans can find help and strength in one another, even though there is no God to assist or guide them. And there are the immense resources and inspirations of nature, that have been celebrated throughout human history, to give succor, help, and peace to human beings—and to do so in the face of the tragedies, inequities, disappointments, and losses that are the inevitable concomitants of finite earthly life.

There is no respite from finitude in religious naturalism's vision of life, and no promise of escape from the perplexities, limitations, and perils of finite life. But religious naturalists can counsel us to consider the seeming sterility and boredom of an alleged afterlife in which there is only eternal peace and the absence of any kind of struggle or need for decision or care, no need for trust or reliance on others or for dealing with accumulating effects of an uncertain future, and no ways in which one's own choices, efforts, or contributions could make any further difference for an already unalterably perfect realm and state of being. Is this not more like an image of *death* rather than of *life* for creatures such as ourselves? Is it not a sort of eternal, effortless, even insentient *requiescat in pace*? This would seem to be a form of life in which there is no need for one's efforts, nothing that one can do to make a difference—because everything is already accomplished. It is not at all clear how, in such an imagined state of unfailing, unblemished, alleged "perfection," one could still be or be allowed to be the same person as one was on earth. One should carefully consider what one wishes for and hopes for, and weigh in the balance the assumed merits and possible demerits of traditional theism's vision of the afterlife.

Of course, this vision is always accompanied by the theistic warning that there is no way in which we can presently picture or imagine such an afterlife. But this claim raises the question of whether it is even a meaningful or desirable hope to be aspired toward. The theistic afterlife is as enigmatic in the final analysis as are many of the avowed traits of the theistic God that might seek to avoid any semblance of a crude anthropomorphism. In the meantime, the religious naturalist is content to assert that to despair of finitude is to despair of the gift of life.

There are aspects of palpable incompleteness, vagueness, and uncertainty in both the traditional theist's and the religious naturalist's visions of the religious life. Whether nature or God is considered as sacred, neither can be expected to be devoid of troublesome perplexity, stupendous wonder, and unfathomable mystery. Claims to absolute epistemic certitude and truth on either side are necessarily vulnerable to serious question. Acknowledgment of this fact should enjoin toleration and respect on both sides of dialogue and debate between the two religious options, and receptiveness to what each of the two sides can contribute to fuller understanding of the other—and not only to better understanding of the other's position, but also to fuller recognition of and further reflection on important aspects of one's own convictional stance. A close-minded, absolutist appeal to special revelation on the part of some theists should not be allowed to stand in the way of such dialogue and debate, given the critical role human interpretation and reason must play in all attempts to interpret and understand the meanings of such putative revelations, especially over large expanses of an elapsed, ever-changing time.

In ending this section's discussion of religious naturalism, I want to call attention to its conception of sin. It is fitting that I do so, for just as Kierkegaard talks of sin "before God," I can talk of sin "before nature." We do not have to look very long or hard in today's world to see the effects of such sins as they affect nature. There are profanations, desecrations, and despoliations of nature resulting from human ignorance, arrogance, and willfulness that are evident on today's earth at every hand. These comprise aspects of the ecological crisis currently confronting the earth.

There are wanton pollutions of earth, sea, and sky. There are extinctions and endangerments of increasing numbers of the creatures of the earth. There are devastating floods, wildfires, storms, sea level rises, ocean acidifications, and global climate changes being brought about by human actions and regretful inactions on today's earth. Our mindless disrespect for the sacredness of nature here on earth is sadly evident everywhere we look. It is producing increasingly untold and undeserved sufferings for human and nonhuman animals alike.

What is the remedy for such egregious and pervasive sins? It is frank acceptance of our human responsibility for them and making every possible effort to stop their downward, increasingly devastating, and destructive effects. Profound repentance for such sins and profound resolve to find effective ways to cease sinning in these ways are humans' hope for redemption in the face of them. We humans also sin against one another in countless deeply regretful ways, despite our each being an aspect of the sacredness of nature. Unsparing efforts and reforms, and feats of imagination and planning of both individual and social kinds are widely needed. There is plenty of desecrating (or desacralizing) sin to go around from the perspective of religion of nature, and no one of us humans is innocent of its commissions and omissions, or immune to its destructive effects.

Both all kinds of sin and of redemption from sin—personal and social—are very much the concern of religious naturalism. The recourse from them lies in our natural gifts as creatures of nature, which are amply adequate in their potential powers for the task. The task has moral, aesthetic, political, scientific, and technical sides, but for the religious naturalist it is also profoundly religious in character. It should be seen as explicitly religious for theists as well, meaning that naturalists and theists must find ways to join hands in a task of common and urgent concern. This is no time to get tied up in issues of differing religious doctrines or beliefs.

Whether mind is primordial or derivative, whether panpsychism is true or false, whether there is or is not a God, there is little uncertainty about what the human mind's principal task should be today for proponents of either side of these issues—in face of the radically threatened condition of today's earth and all of its creatures, human and nonhuman alike. If a giant boulder were suddenly seen to be rolling with ominously accelerating speed toward them by two people hiking on a mountainside, that would not be the time for cantankerous debate between them about whether the boulder is igneous or metamorphic. It is the time to take immediate action in the face of an imminent peril.

Before bringing this final chapter to an end prior to its concluding summary, I want to take a brief look at a topic that is, I believe, highly germane to the themes of this book. This topic is an aspect of the philosophy of the magnificent fourth-century BCE Greek philosopher Aristotle, and the continuing relevance of his philosophy to debate over the concept of panpsychism.

Aristotle, Teleology, and God

On reflection, I am inclined to believe that much of the motive for believing in panpsychism, quite apart from the reasons that might be produced in its defense, is the relatively unexamined assumption that the universe is a single whole and that, as such, it serves some kind of single end or purpose. This end or purpose gives unity and ultimate significance to the universe and, by implication, to human life. This motive for belief in panpsychism is thus primarily *existential*, and not merely *rational*. Views of the universe such as those of Buchler, Cahoone, and William James's *A Pluralistic Universe*, where the so-called *universe* has the pervasive character of actually being a *pluriverse* or *multiverse*, are implicitly discounted and set aside. It must all add up to something, to some final, all-encompassing reason for being, is the tacit assumption. Otherwise, our human lives as parts of the universe would be stripped of meaning.

We can see something like this assumption operating in Aristotle's conception of the Unmoved Mover as the goal of every aspect of the universe. It is also operative in the supremacy given to Plato's Form of the Good, but I want to focus here on Aristotle. The Unmoved Mover in Aristotle's philosophy is not a kind of supreme personal being or God, at least as I interpret it, although it has often been interpreted as such. Instead, it is the actuality, form, property, or universal of the world as a whole. Everything in the world is oriented toward it and imitates it so far as is possible for particular aspects of the world. The life careers of organisms, the rhythms of the seasons, the regular circuits of the planets—all of the observed regularities of the universe—subserve by their imitations the final end, goal, or actuality of the form of the Unmoved Mover. This form constitutes the ultimate unity of the world as a whole, what it is when seen as a single dependable, orderly, predictable system. As such, the Unmoved Mover is not only the form of the world. It is also the final *aition* or "factor responsible for," the world. That is, it is the end served and exhibited by everything in the world. It is the pure, unchanging, and unchangeable actuality on which all the changing actualities of the world depend and to which they are subordinate.

It is ironic that the ultimate truth and reality of the universe is for Aristotle as it was for Plato something believed to be purely actual that is also disembodied. The Unmoved Mover has no material aspect. It is wholly free of all obstructions, encumbrances, and limitations of matter. As alleged pure form or idea, it would seem to be a mere abstraction. But Aristotle gives to it the status of what is most completely real. Thus the more abstract something is, the more real it is in his philosophy, a notable retention of Platonism in it, despite its bringing Plato's philosophy down to earth in so many other ways.

In the medieval theological appropriations of the thought of Aristotle, this final cause, factor, or principle was transmuted into God. It became a personal being instead of being seen simply as the *entelecheia*, "actuality," or form of the universe as a whole, or the regularly functioning aspects of the universe seen comprehensively. Aristotle's forms, like those of Plato, are the knowable aspects of things, and in Aristotle's case they constitute what is actual about them, in contrast with their material *aitia*, which are the aspects of anything that constitute their potentialities, in contrast with their actualities, for being so-instantiated or informed.

Eckhart assumes without question the Aristotelian (and Platonic) idea that the actuality of anything consists in its universal form, quality, idea, or property, not in its material embodiment. This idea can be seen clearly in the following passage from his essay *On the Noble Man*: "The masters say that the power through which the eye sees is quite different from that through which it knows that it sees. The former, the seeing, is something which it takes from the colour rather than from that which is coloured. Thus it is of no consequence whether that which is coloured is a stone or a piece of wood, a person or an angel: *the essential thing* is only that it has colour" (Eckhart 1994: 106, my italics). The actuality of a thing is thus its form, that is, its color in this instance. This color can characterize many different kinds of embodied things and is more actual than any of those things taken singly or collectively. In similar fashion, by virtue of Eckhart's assumption of the superior actuality of form, God as Pure Form is the actuality of the world and thus superior to the world viewed as a whole or to any particular entity or class of entities in the world.

Eckhart's touted mysticism is closely connected with this idea because its implication is that the actuality of the world, namely, God, is—as Pure Form—the ultimate Reality of the universe as a whole and, further, is the *only* Reality from which the world and everything in it flows, to which it returns, and therefore *finally and actually is*. In other words, multiplicity is a delusion and only the One (*to hen*) or God is truly actual. True blessedness consists not so much in knowing intellectually this to be true as in *experiencing* its truth in the depths of one's being (106–07). The world not only stems in its entirety from God and has God as its highest reality and ultimate purpose for being. It is *only* God, a kind of projection, as it were, from the mind of God.

This conviction that everything without exception is *all and only* the Divine Mind is a type of extreme panpsychism. It is the conclusion that *psyche*, that is, spirit or mind, is not only *pan*, in the sense of *always and everywhere*, but even more fundamentally that it is the *sole* reality. In other words, everything is mind, and only mind.

Moreover, the Divine Mind, for Eckhart as for most of the theologians of the medieval period, is timeless or outside of time. The passage of time is thus ultimately an illusion, as is any kind of evolutionary change. Eckhart writes, "When we say 'man,' then this word also signifies that which is above nature, above time, and above everything which leans toward time or itself smacks of time, and the same is true with respect to space and corporeality" (105). He has in mind, of course, the *universal form of man*, not any particular human being. The contrast between this conviction of Eckhart and my own claim to the primordiality of matter-energy and time is quite apparent.

Because reality for Aristotle lies solely in forms (or universals), not in matter, the Unmoved Mover's perfection consists in its being entirely actual with no semblance or limit of potentiality or change. Seen in this way, we can readily understand medieval theologians' readiness to see it as a personal, purposeful, living God and to view that God as giving purpose to the world as a whole and to each human life. We can easily also comprehend why such a belief had profound existential, and not merely theoretical, import for medieval Christians and why it has such import for many contemporary Christians—as well as for many Jews and Muslims—today. God, seen as pure spirit, is analogous to the Unmoved Mover as pure actuality. The query of the 1966 movie *Alfie*, "What's it all about?," strongly suggests that the universe, viewed as an "all" or as a single whole system, has to be *about* or to *add up* finally to something. Hence, panpsychism has to be true, because only pervasive, underived mind can give purpose and meaning to everything assumed to be contained within a primordially *purposive* and thus ultimately *reassuring* world.

It is also important to note in this connection that Aristotle's world is a static, unchanging world. He knows nothing of the idea of evolution that is so central to our understanding of the world today. Evolution shows us how crucial the idea of change is to our current view of the universe. Because for us today, informed by a scientific view of reality, the universe is constantly undergoing change, new things are constantly coming into being and old things are passing out of being. The universe exhibits a constantly evolving, novel, irreducible *manyness*, therefore, and not a consistent, unchanging unity of *sameness*. And among the uncountably many new things it evolves and exhibits on earth are conscious beings like us, with our consciously entertained and projected purposes. Purposes evolve, therefore, rather than being primordial. This is the heart of my critique of panpsychistic teleology.

There may be, as I strongly believe, no discernible purpose of the universe, but there are many kinds of purpose or end-directed behaviors in it on the part of each of its evolved and continually evolving life forms, and especially those capable of conscious purposes and purposing. The universe is uncountably many things, and these things exhibit both connections and disconnections in their relations with one another. There is no purpose of the universe as a whole partly because there is no such thing as a single, unitary, unchanging universe. And teleology and purpose are emergent phenomena in living beings, not something preexisting or primordial. This is my central conviction and this book's central thesis.

Conclusion

In this chapter, I have compared and contrasted two kinds of religious faith, namely, theism and religious naturalism. In doing so, I have emphasized the existential import of these two kinds of faith, and not just differences in their conceptual systems. For the theist, everything is ultimately related to and focused on God. For the religious naturalist, the focus is fixed finally on nature. Each of these perspectives outlines not only a way of thinking but a whole way of life. When we consider panpsychism in the context of these two perspectives, we can recognize its profound importance for the theist, an importance it does not have for the religious naturalist.

For the theist, the purposes of God are paramount. God is a spiritual being who has purposefully created the universe and everything in it, including matter-energy and time. God's purposes continue to order the world as a whole. Mind or spirit is thus primordial, not derivative. In contrast to this view of reality, the religious naturalist is content to regard mind and purpose as the outcomes of ongoing evolutionary processes over extraordinarily long spans of time, and as the property, initially, of emergent living beings of all kinds and then in increasingly conscious forms as the varieties of these living forms continue to evolve. And they evolve as products of the interactions of uncreated matter-energy with endless time. Thus in the one case, everything is oriented toward God, while in the other, everything is oriented toward nature.

Moreover, while theism is convinced that the universe as a whole is created, ordered, and ruled by God, the religious naturalist does not see the universe as an ordered whole that contains everything, but as an extremely complex system of orders, none of which is either contained by or contains everything else. The universe is, more properly, then, conceived as a plethora of orders rather than as a single, all-encompassing order. It is actually a pluriverse or multiverse rather than a universe. No single system of it encompasses all other systems, although there are multiple intersections and interactions of particular systems of it with one another. There is no purpose of the whole either antecedent to it or characteristic of it.

But there are ample purposes within its living creatures, including our continuously felt, thought about, and acted upon purposes as human beings. Denial of primordial purpose does not preempt or make inexplicable the presence of multiple real purposes and purposive activities on earth. Nor does it make them any less meaningful and important. Teleology need not be primordial in order to have vast, all-pervading significance among the life forms of the earth, including our own life form as humans.

In the last section of this chapter, I ruminated on the philosophy of Aristotle and the influence at least semblances of it have had, since the High Middle Ages, on the theistic thought of the West. Aristotle's Pure Form or Unmoved Mover, viewed as the final *aition* of the universe envisioned as a whole, was interpreted in the Middle Ages as the purposeful creator and sustainer, God. Seen as such, the universe was comprehended as a whole, and that whole as ordered, governed, and guided everywhere by the will and purpose of God. God is therefore the origin, focus, and ultimate purpose of what is rightly to be regarded as a universe, and not merely as a pluriverse, meaning that purpose, and the divine mind capable of purposive intent and action are primordial, lying behind and directing everything that exists. Hence, panpsychism of the theistic, or more properly, monotheistic kind, lies at the heart of the universe.

There are commonalities and overlaps of thought and practice of these two religious outlooks, to be sure, but their ontologies or metaphysics are fundamentally different. Panpsychism is also fundamentally different ontologically or metaphysically from the emergentist account of purpose and purposiveness I have devoted this book to defending. I do not argue that monotheism is the *sole source* of panpsychism, because it clearly is not. But I do want to point to the considerable influence versions of theistic religious thought in the Western hemisphere have long had and continue to have on the panpsychist view, whether such influence is explicitly endorsed or only tacitly assumed and subconsciously active.

Different roots can produce similar fruits. I do not want for a moment to gainsay the enormous amount of good that can be done in the world by theists, theistic panpsychists, and nontheistic panpsychists. I take issue in this book not with the commendable practices that may be inspired by their beliefs but only with the adequacy and convincingness of their conceptual schemes, just as they will no doubt take issue in similar fashion with mine. But whether purpose is primordial or derivative, there would be no point in denying its reality and great importance. What is of supreme importance is that we humans think, plan, and act with careful consideration for the habitats, lives, and worthy purposes of others, whether these others be human or nonhuman.

Good personal purposes support good lives, lives of mercy, justice, and helpfulness to others as well as to oneself. And they are deeply needed for the production and maintenance of just and equitable human societies. Bad, misguided, thoughtless purposes can have opposite effects, not only for human beings but for the natural world throughout the earth. In this chapter I called attention in this connection to the dire ecological situation of our earth today. This situation gives frightful witness to the effects of bad purposes and the absence of well-thought-out and intelligently implemented good purposes.

Theists can join hands with religious naturalists in such respects, for the basic thrust of their respective forms of faith is existential, that is, its effects on practice. Neither of the two is simply a mental parlor game, and debate between them is not merely a matter of detached, largely irrelevant intellectual disagreement. I should not want to deny the importance of right thinking that is held responsive to available and pertinent evidence. It is my assumed purpose as a philosopher to encourage such thinking and perhaps in some small ways to contribute to its development and advancement. Thoughts, beliefs, ideas, and conceptual schemes are important because they can prepare the way to actions, and actions—especially actions of the consciously purposive and strenuous kind—can lead to beneficial practical effects.

It is important, therefore, for us to think as clearly, accurately, and perceptively as we can in addressing the origin, nature, status, and the best, most effective roles of purposes in our actions and in our conceptions of ourselves and our world. The gem at the center of consciousness is its capacity for carefully deliberated purposive action. This capacity is wondrous and crucial enough to warrant our thoughtful questioning, consideration of opposing positions, and sustained attention regarding it.

Notes

Chapter Two. Two Meanings of *Telos*

1. To say this is not at this point to take issue with the Second Law of Thermodynamics because usable energy is admittedly expended in emergent processes. But will all of the available usable energy eventually be used up? That depends on whether the present universe or face of nature is a closed system and the one and only universe. I do not believe that it is a causally closed or deterministic system. I also endorse the idea of an everlasting succession of physical universes, each emerging from and transforming the remnants of a previous one, and each eventually becoming the basis of another one over endless time. Usable matter-energy in this way can be reconstituted, reexpressed, or recycled but never finally used up. There is thus no origin or ending of dynamic matter-energy itself or of time.

I am convinced that all process involves both continuity and novelty, and that without these two factors change of any kind would be impossible. The fundamental and inexpungeable role I assign to novelty as a necessary aspect of the flow of time is incompatible with the Second Law of Thermodynamics, which seems to assume and require causal determinism leading to an inevitable collapse of all further process or change. Moreover, the primordial status of time, for which I argue, means that there can be no such thing as either or an origin or an ending of time. The Second Law and its implications are complicated topics that would require detailed philosophical discussion and argument and carry us too far afield of the concerns of this chapter.

2. This is the sense in which Evan Thompson uses the term *purpose* when he attributes it to all of life.

Chapter Three. Teleology and Values

1. Evan Thompson views these three traits as constituting the presence of *mind* in all living things, as we saw in chapter 1. This usage chimes in with White-

head's term *mentality*, which he appears to assume as belonging to all life in some degree, as shown in the epigraph of the present chapter. Mindful life in this sense can be unconscious as well as conscious, and there are many different degrees of consciousness among a large number of the kinds of life on earth.

2. David Hume famously argued that it would be a non sequitur fallacy to reason from an observed fact (a descriptive "is") to some kind of prescriptive injunction (an "ought"). Oxford philosopher G. E. Moore argued in the early twentieth century that such reasoning is a commission of what he termed "the naturalistic fallacy." The "good," he explained, is indefinable and its nature cannot be deduced from a description of any existing state of affairs that is not already assumed to have the character of value or to contain aspects of value (Hume 1980, III, 1: 1, 469–70; Moore 1993: 62–69).

3. I provide a different and more detailed discussion of natural values in chapter 4 of *A Religion of Nature* (2002) and discuss explicitly *religious* natural values in part 4 of that book. The four natural values I discuss in this chapter are meant only to be illustrative of the presence of values in nature or, more specifically, of their presence as potentially valuable ends for human contemplation, appreciation, incorporation, and action as creatures of nature.

4. In my book *Primordial Time*, I take strong issue with the notion that time itself has come into being with the Big Bang origin of the present universe and that it will end with a supposed entropic "heat death" of this universe, in accordance with the Second Law of Thermodynamics (see especially pages 35–37 of that book).

Chapter Seven. Teleology and Two Kinds of Religious Faith

1. The unfamiliar terms *potentiate* and *potentiated*, in this translation of Kierkegaard's Danish writing, I judge to mean something like "make possible" and "made possible."

2. See Arthur O. Lovejoy's book by this title. Medieval developments of the great chain of being idea had their roots in the philosophies of Plato, Aristotle, and Plotinus.

Works Cited

Ackerman, Jennifer. 2017. *The Genius of Birds*. New York: Penguin Books.

Aristotle. 1941a. *On the Parts of Animals*, translated by William Ogle. In *The Basic Works of Aristotle*, edited by Richard McKeon, 641–61. New York: Random House.

———. 1941b. *Physics*, translated by R. P. Hardie and R. K. Gaye. In *The Basic Works of Aristotle*, edited by Richard McKeon, 218–394. New York: Random House.

Augustine. 1961. *The Confessions of Saint Augustine*. New York: Collier Books.

Buchler, Justus. 1990. *Metaphysics of Natural Complexes: Second Expanded Edition*. Edited by Kathleen Wallace and Armen Marsoobian, with Robert S. Corrington. Albany: State University of New York Press.

Cahoone, Lawrence. 2019. "Aristotle and Whitehead: Emergence, Process, and the Importance of Irrelevance." In *Conceiving an Alternative: Philosophical Resources for an Ecological Civilization*, edited by Demian Wheeler and David E. Conner, 169–84. Anoka, MN: Process Century Press.

———. 2013. *The Orders of Nature*. Albany: State University of New York Press.

Conner, David E. 2019. "Beyond Emergentism." In *Conceiving an Alternative: Philosophical Resources for an Ecological Civilization*, edited by Demian Wheeler and David E. Conner, 185–228. Anoka, MN: Process Century Press.

Crosby, Donald A. 2022a. *Sacred and Secular: Responses to Life in a Finite World*. Albany: State University of New York Press.

———. 2022b. *The Multiplicity of Interpreted Worlds: Inner and Outer Perspectives*. Lanham, MD: Lexington Books.

———. 2020. *Primordial Time: Its Irreducible Reality, Human Significance, and Ecological Import*. Lanham, MD: Lexington Books.

———. 2016. "Probabilism, Emergentism, and Pluralism: A Naturalistic Metaphysics of Radical Materialism." *American Journal of Theology and Philosophy* 37, no. 3: 216–27.

———. 2013. *The Philosophy of William James: Radical Empiricism and Radical Materialism*. Lanham, MD: Rowman & Littlefield.

———. 2002. *A Religion of Nature*. Albany: State University of New York Press.

Dawkins, Richard. 1987. *The Blind Watchmaker: Why the Evidence of Evolution Reveals a Universe without Design*. New York: W. W. Norton.

Dennett, Daniel C. 2004. *Freedom Evolves*. New York: Penguin Books.

———. 1991. *Consciousness Explained*. New York: Little, Brown.

Dewey, John. 1981. "Morality Is Social." In *The Philosophy of John Dewey*, edited by John J. McDermott, 712–23. Chicago: University of Chicago Press.

Eckhart, Johannes. 1994. *Meister Eckhart: Selected Writings*. Translated and edited by Oliver Davies. New York: Penguin Books.

Feinberg, Todd E., and Jon E. Mallatt. 2018. *Consciousness Demystified*. Cambridge, MA: MIT Press.

Gould, Stephen Jay. 1989. *Wonderful Life*. New York: W. W. Norton.

The Holy Bible. 1962. Revised Standard Version. Edited by Herbert G. May and Bruce M. Metzger. New York: Oxford University Press.

Hume, David. 1980. *A Treatise of Human Nature*, second edition. Edited by L. A. Selby-Bigge and P. H. Nidditch. Oxford: Clarendon Press.

James, William. 1977. *A Pluralistic Universe*. Cambridge, MA: Harvard University Press.

Kierkegaard, Søren. 1951. *The Sickness unto Death*. Translated by Walter Lowrie. Princeton, NJ: Princeton University Press.

Koch, Christof. 2021. "The Brain Electric: Electrodes that Stimulate Brain Tissue Reveal the Topography of Conscious Experience." *Scientific American*, June 1, 71–75.

Leidenhag, Mikael. 2021. *Naturalizing God? A Critical Evaluation of Religious Naturalism*. Albany: State University of New York Press.

———. 2019. "Does Naturalism Make Room for Teleology? The Case of Donald Crosby and Thomas Nagel." *American Journal of Theology and Philosophy* 40, no. 1: 5–19.

Lewis, C. S. 1955. *Surprised by Joy: The Shape of My Early Life*. New York: Harcourt, Brace, Jovanovich.

Lovejoy, Arthur O. 1976. *The Great Chain of Being: A Study of the History of an Idea*. Cambridge, MA: Harvard University Press.

Luther, Martin. 1943. "A Treatise on Christian Liberty," translated by W. A. Lambert. In *Three Treatises by Martin Luther*, 252–90. Philadelphia, PA: Muhlenberg Press.

McKibben, Bill. 2021. "The World Speeds Up—and We Slow Down: Climate Destruction Is Now Moving Much Faster than Human Institutions." *The Climate Crisis*, the *New Yorker*'s newsletter on the environment, June 30. https://www.newyorker.com/news/annals-of-a-warming-planet-/the-world-speeds-up-and-we-slow-down.

Moore, G. E. 1993. *Principia Ethica*, revised edition. Edited by Thomas Baldwin. Cambridge, UK: Cambridge University Press.

Nagel, Thomas. 2012. *Mind and Cosmos: Why the Materialist, Neo-Darwinian Conception of Nature Is Almost Certainly False.* New York: Oxford University Press.

Niebuhr, Reinhold. 1949. *The Nature and Destiny of Man: A Christian Interpretation.* New York: Charles Scribner's Sons.

Otto, Rudolf. 1958. *The Idea of the Holy: An Inquiry into the Non-rational Factor in the Idea of the Divine and Its Relation to the Rational.* Translated by John W. Harvey. New York: A Galaxy Book, Oxford University Press.

Paumgarten, Nick. 2021. "What a Feeling: Energy and How to Get It." *New Yorker*, November 8, 18–24.

Randall, John Herman, Jr. 1960. *Aristotle.* New York: Columbia University Press.

Raymo, Chet. 2008. *When God Is Gone, Everything Is Holy: The Making of a Religious Naturalist.* Notre Dame, IN: Sorin Books.

Safina, Carl. 2020. *Becoming Wild: How Animal Cultures Raise Families, Create Beauty, and Achieve Peace.* New York: Henry Holt.

Sartre, Jean-Paul. 1948. *Existentialism and Humanism.* Translated by Philip Mairet. Brooklyn, NY: Haskell House.

Taylor, Charles. 1964. *The Explanation of Behaviour.* London: Routledge & Kegan Paul.

Thompson, Evan. 2007. *Mind in Life: Biology, Phenomenology, and the Sciences of Mind.* Cambridge, MA: Belknap Press of Harvard University Press.

Wheeler, Demian. 2018. "Deus Sive Natura: Pantheism as a Variety of Religious Naturalism." In *The Routledge Handbook of Religious Naturalism*, edited by Donald A. Crosby and Jerome A. Stone, 106–17. London: Routledge.

Whitehead, Alfred North. 1975. *Process and Reality: An Essay in Cosmology*, corrected edition. Edited by David Ray Griffin and Donald W. Sherburne. New York: Free Press.

———. 1958. *Modes of Thought.* New York: Capricorn Books.

Index

Tillich, Paul, 64
time, 2
  in relation to defense of
    panpsychism, 96–97
  and origination of mind from
    matter, 90–91
transformation, 35
Treatise on Christian Liberty (Luther),
  125

ultimate authority, sources of, 82–84
unconscious life, 80–81
universe, purpose of, 139–42
universe, sacred majesty of, 69–72
Unmoved Mover, 44, 140–42

values, 52–55
  disvalues, 67

earth, 67–69
other-value, 65–67
sacred majesty of the universe,
  69–72S
sea, 67–69
self-value, 63–65
sky, 67–69
telic values, 73–86
teleological character of, 60–61
teleology and, 59–72
ultimate source of, 61–63
vector character, 59

Whitehead, Alfred North, 7, 28, 59,
  113
  metaphysics of, 35–36

zygote, 97